ACCORDING TO PURPOSE

God's Providence as seen in the Book of Esther

by
Rev. A. A. Campbell, BA

As the providence of God doth, in general, reach to all creatures; so, after a most special manner, it taketh care of his Church, and disposeth all things to the good thereof.

(Westminster Confession of Faith)

Edited and Published by
N. A. Campbell, CEng.

5 Strathearn Park, Belfast BT4 2GN

First Published 1988

—

© *N. A. Campbell, 1988*

—

—

ISBN 0 9513769 0 X

—

Printed and bound in Northern Ireland by The Manley Group Ltd., Belfast

ACCORDING TO PURPOSE

CONTENTS

FOREWARD

The Shorter Catechism states that "God's works of providence are his most holy, wise and powerful preserving and governing all his creatures, and all their actions" (Ans. 11).

Modern life often seems so complex and bewildering, without purpose. Our lives appear to be influenced from all sides by governments, big business, war and terrorism. God is usually forgotten and the Christian's voice ignored.

However, the Bible puts a different view on events. As the Shorter Catechism implies, God is in control whether individuals and organisations acknowledge Him or not. This book, through a study of the Book of Esther, a book in which God is not mentioned once, seeks to give an understanding of the Doctrine of Providence set out in Scripture and to apply it to Christian life in the modern world.

N. A. Campbell

ACCORDING TO PURPOSE

I

GOD HAS A PLAN

Life is most complex, bewildering, perplexing. There seems little pattern or rhyme and reason to it. War, violence, industrial strife both at home and abroad destroy or nullify what man has built for himself. Such activities are deplored and abhorred by the majority. Having tasted their bitter fruits we resolve never again to be tormented by them, but they continue; we are seemingly unable to profit from the mistakes of earlier days and past generations. The decision of politicians and economists, even in countries far distanced from ours, affect our standard of living, as also the customs, fashions and ethics in places afar off have a bearing upon, and often alter, our moral standards. There is conflict between religion and no-religion; religion is against religion and philosophy against philosophy, each claiming to be the truth and on the way to ultimate reality, while decrying or discrediting the others. We are born and eventually die, and in between both events which are determined for us, we live and learn, work and play, know joy and sorrow, find ourselves co-operating with or being opposed to others, profess confidence in one creed while disowning and perhaps scoffing at others and, finally, leaving this scene are soon forgotten and are as though we had never been. This fate is the lot even of the most famous and influential. Life scarcely seems worth all the fuss and bother associated with it. Yet, those who thought like that gave birth to us and we in turn give birth to others. We live and we want to live, struggle not to die, and grieve when even the least among us expires. So it has been since the beginnings of human history. Is there a pattern and purpose to such a life? The sceptic and the cynic deny it. Some view man as a superior being, an angel born to be free, but fated to spend his existence in chains to no purpose; others think of him as a spartan character who unflinchingly takes the worst that chance or misfortune can throw at him, and yet is the determiner and controller of his own destiny, though that destiny be not stated explicitly. Many regard man as a unique kind of animal whose only business is to eat, drink and be merry, to draw from life all that is sensuous and sensual before he departs and is no more; while not a few claim that the perpetuating of the human race is the chief end of man, consider they have lived, if they contribute to its continuance and make the world what they consider to be a slightly better place for their offspring; though fully aware that their successors might destroy or abuse what material, aesthetic or ethical advances they might make.

But mixing among the masses of mankind there is a kingdom, a kingdom which is not confined to any one language or territory, has infiltrated all nations, expresses itself in the tongues and through the cultures of the peoples where it finds itself. A kingdom which is tolerated or objected to, is encouraged or opposed according to the temper or the material, political or religious philosophy of the community or nation in whose midst it is. It has been reduced again and again to a pitifully small remnant, yet has never been destroyed. It is a kingdom without any visible head, yet owes allegiance to one great King, is submissive to His law and ever strives to practice the spiritual, ethical and moral wisdom which is its charter, and to walk in the way of life mapped out for it. This wisdom and way are among its most outstanding features, making it unique among the groupings of mankind in the world. It is the kingdom of God. Its King is Jesus Christ the crucified. Its symbol is a cross. Its expectation, that all the kingdoms of this world shall become the kingdom of God and His Christ. Its purpose, to labour by means of the law of its King and in the spirit of His life to see that expectation realised. Its hope is to live and reign eternally with its invisible Head when this purpose has been achieved. This is the kingdom which views the world's stage with enlightened eyes, sees it in the light shed by the law of the great King. The truth it sees, confirmed by history and personal experience, permits its members to trace a pattern in life which convinces them that all things are working together for good to them that love God, to them that are called according to purpose. This world-view is based on the revelation given by the King and their faith in it. It teaches them that their King lives for ever, that His dominion is an everlasting dominion, His kingdom is from generation to generation, before Whom all the inhabitants of the earth are as nothing. He works according to His will in the armies of heaven and among the inhabitants of the earth. None can stay His hand or say to Him, ''What are you doing?'' That is, the citizens of this kingdom are convinced that all the bewilderment and perplexity, all the confusion and uncertainty, all that is evil and abhorrent, together with all that is thrilling, delightful, pleasant, right and true are allies working together in mysterious harmony under the hand of the great King to produce the final, eternal triumph of good over evil, right over wrong, righteousness over injustice, love over hatred, thereby bringing great glory to Himself. It is the triumph of His kingdom which He Himself has planned and in the way He has planned it. The name given to the pattern by which the plan is worked out is called the Providence of God.

The Westminster Confession of Faith under the heading, The decree of God, states, ''God from all eternity did, by the most wise and holy counsel of His own will, freely and unchangeably ordain whatsoever comes to pass, yet so, as thereby God is neither the author of sin, nor is violence offered to the will of the creature, nor is the liberty or contingency of second causes taken away, but rather established''. And it goes on to say that God began to put this decree into effect by the work of creation, and is making it effective by means of His Providence. By Providence the Confession means that ''God, the creator of all things, doth uphold, direct, dispose and govern all creatures, actions and things, from the greatest even to the least, by His most wise and holy providence, according to His infallible foreknowledge, and the free and immutable counsel of His own will, to the praise of the glory of His wisdom, power, justice, goodness and mercy''. That is a concise and fair summary of the teaching of the Bible on the subject of Providence. The Bible is known to the members of the kingdom as the Word of God, the law of God by which entrance into and life within the kingdom is governed. The Book of Esther, one of the historical books of the Bible, is a living enactment of this doctrine of the Providence of God.

On the face of it the Book of Esther might not seem the ideal choice from which to seek an understanding of so vital a truth as the doctrine before us. It is one of two books in the Old Testament from which the name of God has been omitted, the Song of Solomon being the other. This has led some to suppose that the work is fictitious, at best an historical novel attempting to account for the instituting of the Feast of Purim (9:17ff), barren of any contribution to the Church's body of divinity. But various reasons may be adduced for this most significant omission, particularly as Esther is a book most loved by, and precious to, the Jews. For example, whoever the author, in all probability he relied heavily on the official records of the reign of Ahasuerus for much of his information (cf.10:2; 6:1) and, obviously, the name and operations of Jehovah would be conspicuous by their absence from such chronicles. More likely, however, being himself an Israelite in whom there was no guile, and addressing himself to Israelites in order to confirm them in the faith of God's elect, the author adopted a style of presentation free from a false or exaggerated pietism which could easily distort the truth, which would concentrate their minds on some of the salient features of a doctrine familiar and dear to them. This illustration of the Providence of God at work was written to reassure his readers that at all times their God reigned and was in complete control of every situation. The reference to fasting in chapter 4, verse 16, always associated in the Jewish mind with the importance and urgency of penitential prayer in a time of crisis, would convince them that God was very much active in the narrative. It was a reminder to them that in times of crisis they were not expected to sit back passively and wait for God to intervene. With Elijah-like prayer (I Kgs.18:42; Jas.2:17) they were to wrestle with God as the One Who must be enquired of by the house of Israel to work for them (Ezek.36:37), and to use their initiative as themselves being instruments of God's purpose. When the Lord is intent on preserving and building up Zion, He appears in His glory and regards the prayerful endeavour of His destitute people (cf.8:17; Ps.102:16,17). In this connection, the author is at pains to show that this truth he is advocating, namely, that God foreordains whatsoever comes to pass and that for His own glory, does not make men puppets or not responsible for their own behaviour. With the name of God omitted, we see men and women acting freely according to their individual charcters, virtues, fears, faith, ambitions, lusts, passions and circumstances, as though there were no God or that He had neither part nor interest in the plot. Following them through their courses of action, we find ourselves applauding the rewarding of the good and the faithful, and assenting to the bringing of evil men to their just desserts. Yet, to that must be added that such is the skill with which the writer tells his story, he convinces us that at each stage of his narrative the coincidences, such as the deposing of Vashti and the accession of Esther to the throne (chpts. 1 & 2), the forgetfulness to honour Mordecai's loyalty to the person of the king and the king's later bout of insomnia (2:21-23; 6:1-3), Haman's visit to the palace to request the execution of Mordecai and his being ordered to organise and lead a procession in honour of the man he hated (5:14; 6:5,6,10,11), Haman building gallows for the destruction of Mordecai and his second invitation to Esther's banquet which led to his execution on the scaffold he had had erected (5:14; 7:1,10), were not chance happenings. They were coincidences because God, Who knows the end from the beginning, Who had decreed the security of His people from all eternity, Who is prepared for every exigency, and Who secretly works all things according to the counsel of His own will, caused them to relate one to the other that His purpose might be attained.

That leads to an obvious fact: the doctrine of Providence found in the Book of Esther is presented not in abstract or academic terms difficult for many to understand, but in the flesh and blood language of national history and human experience. Here we are introduced to real people, men and women who, though belonging to a different time, place and culture, having perhaps a different status in society and very much the creatures of their day, yet are men and women of like passions with ourselves. The ambition, jealousy, pride, humility, greed, fear, love, hate, loyalty, patriotism, intrigue, insatiable desire for revenge, triumph and defeat, sorrow and joy, which we know to be common to man and typical of any nation or community which has ever been or is likely to be, are pictured for us in life sized characters. As the drama unfolds, we see the cast in their relations with each other, are aware of the motives which spur each individual, and how by their actions, reactions and counteractions each and all are being led on toward a planned end. But more: as we read, the scenario and the personnel fade and we see our own day and situation, find ourselves in the stead of Esther and Mordecai, and the Jews become the Church. It is our story. We are seeing it in prevision, as those who have the mind of God and are seated together with Christ in the heavenlies. We see the end from the beginning and know that the end is planned. Mercifully, the precise details are spared us, but the confidence the history inspires is that whatever the trauma in our lives, whatever the ups and downs of life, however much our way of life might twist and turn, the destination for which we hope will be reached, the pattern of life we strive after will be attained. They will be reached and attained because the green pastures and living waters, the hills and the dales, the diversions and the dark valleys which mark our road are the only way to the Father's house; and we are given the confidence that all the happiness this way gives, and all the pain and scars it inflicts upon us are the discipline which is making us what the Father wants us to be. And this we shall be when, reaching journey's end, we see Jesus as He is and are made like Him.

Were the Book of Esther the only Biblical source of the Providence of God illustrated from the lives and experiences of both godly and ungodly men and women, we might be accused of reading into it what the narrative does not contain. But doctrine taught by means of the biographies of the faithful and others is one of the outstanding features of the Scriptures. Projected on to the screen of divine revelation in all their humanness, weaknesses as well as strengths, vices as well as virtues, lapses together with advances, these characters epitomise the truthfulness, beauty and grace of the doctrines the Holy Spirit would instruct us in. The Epistle to the Hebrews chapter 11 can be claimed as our warrant for making that assertion. From that portion we gather that faith is the invisible spiritual driving force which makes the Christian life possible and its blessings realities (v.1). How difficult then to speak of the doctrine of faith in concrete terms, unless illustrated by living examples of it in action. This the writer of the Hebrews does. He places before us miniature portraits of some of the outstanding saints of the Old Testament, so exemplifying one or more facets of faith, and when we turn back to the full length portraits of these same individuals as found in the Old Testament gallery, we learn from their example, their failures and successes what faith is. The Apostle Paul adopted a similar method of teaching faith. In Romans chapter 3 we have his instruction on the great theme of justification by faith introduced, and in order to safeguard against being misunderstood and to make his meaning perfectly clear, he goes on in chapter 4 to illustrate the truth from the life and practice of Abraham. Similarly, when in Second Corinthians chapter 5, Paul expounds the glory of gospel power, he says, "If any man be in Christ Jesus, he is a new creation; old things are passed away; behold, all things have become new" (v.17). This is a saying hard to be understood, unless he himself is speaking from personal experience, and a change has taken place in him which all who knew him previously can recognise. Frequently, he spoke of the transformation which had taken place in his life on the Damascus Road and which became more pronounced with the passing of the years (see Acts 9:1-22; 22:1-16; 26:1-19; Philp.3:3-12; I Tim.1:12-15 etc.). This was a change many could verify. It was one of the reasons why he suffered so much at the hands of his former friends. They did not like what they saw because it condemned their way of life. He never spoke of this change outwith the context of what the gospel of Jesus Christ can do; used it always to say in effect, "I am what it means to be a 'new creation in Christ Jesus''. The changed life exemplified the doctrine. So we could go on, but sufficient has been said to prove the point. Scripture reveals that while the Lord God considered it necesary and important to teach His theology by means of sermon and homily, exhortation and precept, poetry and prophecy, yet always He was careful to sketch the truth with examples from the testimony of history and individual experience, saying, as he set the testimony before the people, "This is what I mean; this is what I do; this is the doctrine. Believe it; receive it; practise it; rest in it, and it will be to you as to my saints of old". And so it is with Providence.

The Book of Esther, then, is but one of the many histories found in the Bible where God, working by means of the free, deliberate, responsible or irresponsible actions of men and women, brings to a happy outcome what He has planned for His people. By two, three and more histories He confirms that Providence is His secret weapon, one He is using without respite, usually in a mysterious and unexpected manner and without the knowledge of the majority of the individuals involved, and which He never employs in vain. Therefore, when tracing the goodness of God to Esther,

Mordecai and their fellow Jews through the labyrinth of courage, intrigue, favour, fear and faith, which we find in the pages of this book, we will have recourse repeatedly to the biographies and experiences of other Scripture characters, to support the claim that neither chance nor luck, as commonly understood, was responsible for the amazing turn of events witnessed there. God was at work, over-seeing, over-ruling and directing all for His glory.

Before turning to the events recorded in Esther, an important feature of Old Testament history as it relates to Providence must be considered; namely, the apparent triviality of many of the incidents narrated. The historical portions of this sacred volume trace the story of Israel from its founding as a nation to the return from exile in Babylon, and contains much which is of national importance and pride to the Jews: God's promise to Abraham and sealed as a covenant; the harrowing experiences of the nation's founding fathers and their immediate successors in Egypt; their miraculous exodus from that land and the forty years sojourn in the wilderness which followed. There in that most unlikely environment the national religion and way of life was established and developed under Moses; then there was the conquest and the inhabiting of Canaan, the formative years of nationhood under a series of Judges, the rise of the monarchy, the progress to international eminence and prosperity during the reigns of David and Solomon, the centralising of religious worship at Jerusalem by the building of Solomon's Temple, the unhappy division of the State when Rehoboam ruled, national and religious decline, exile in Babylon and the ultimate return of the people to their homeland and the restoration of national life in the days of Ezra and Nehemiah. As with all nations, a past in which there is much to be both proud and ashamed of. But there are many strange omissions from this record. The greater part of the time spent in the wilderness is passed over in comparative silence, as though it were of no importance whatever (cf. Num.33:1-49). The formative period prior to the monarchy is largely unrecorded. Decades are glossed over with nothing more than the mention of a judge's name, perhaps with the addition of what might seem an eccentricity (Jud.10:3-5). Some of the kings are dismissed with no mention of their reigns, other than that they were either good or bad and the mentioning of their mothers' names. Obviously, the Old Testament does not pretend to be an historian's chronicle of Israel and its neighbours. Those who want that are directed to other sources (I Chron.29:29,30; II Chron.9:29; 12:15; Esth.10:1,2 etc.). Included are narratives of the experiences and doings of individuals, many of which scarcely seem worthy of a mention or are of little national interest or importance and better forgotten. For example, a great number of words is used to narrate the misdemeanours of Abraham, Jacob, David and the like, the amours of Samson and Solomon, the choosing of a bride for Isaac, the romance of Ruth and Boaz, and the lack of intelligence shown by a nameless Levite and its tragic consequences (Judges 19 - 21). The list of such events, experiences and anecdotes which fills the pages of the Old Testament is a long one, and are what historians would term trivia. The explanation is simple. The Old Testament is the unique revelation of the founding, forming, developing, and preserving of the kingdom of God on the earth. Its authenticity and authority is that it claims, and is proved to be, the word of God. Each and every part of it is "God-breathed" (II Tim.3:16); that is, God communicated direct to His penmen what should be recorded, using their individual minds and wills, intelligence, education, powers of observation, deduction, and their environment and so on, when doing so, that there might be a complete and inerrant record of His purpose and power preserved in writing for posterity (II Pet.1:21; cf. Ex.17:14; Jer.30:2; Dan.12:4). It is "the word of the Lord which endures for ever" (I Pet.1:25), the word which cannot be removed, erased or destroyed (see Jer.36:1-32).

The purpose of the revelation was to make known what the covenant purpose of God is, namely, the calling out of the world of a people who would form His kingdom (Gen.12:1-3; 15:5,6; cf. I Pet.2:9), what its foundations and functions are, how entrance into it is made, and its consummation in His Messiah, the Lord Jesus Christ. Further, the historical and biographical content of the Old Testament, with which we are concerned principally, was chosen by the discriminating Spirit of truth to illustrate for, and ever keep before, the citizens of the kingdom, the faithfulness, steadfastness, wisdom and power of God at work, keeping His covenant and perfecting that which concerns His people, individually and collectively, whatever they or others might do. Every incident and narrative recorded, whatever its content, whether it pictures men and women in their strengths or weaknesses, or a mixture of both, and whether they be working for or against His covenant purposes, when seen in the light of God's overall plan, is pregnant with the truth that God is there overseeing and over-ruling. Without respite, He intervened in every situation, protecting and advancing His own people and His designs for them. Regarding this, there are two significant features of God's interventions which should not be overlooked. The individuals involved, particularly those opposed to or heedless of God's covenant and kingdom, are unaware that He is using what they do and say against them and for His own ends; and, always His interventions are timely, apt and successful in their unobtrusiveness. Men, being unaware of His workings, cannot negate them. Sometimes His interventions on behalf of His kingdom were by the birth, preservation, upbringing and future work of a child - Isaac, Moses, Samson, Obed, Solomon, to name but a few - and all pointing toward the birth and work of God's holy child, Jesus. At other times, He used the duplicity of unprincipled men, Jacob supplanting Esau, and then inveigled into polygamy, first by Laban, his father-in-law, and then by the jealousies of the two sisters who were his wives. On occasion it was the lustfulness of such as Samson and David the Lord over-ruled to further the interests of His kingdom. And often the unexpected happened, as when two starving lepers went to the besieging Assyrian camp to beg for food, only to discover that the army had returned hurriedly to their own land, leaving their stores behind. Thus, did the Lord relieve the beleaguered, famine ridden city of Samaria (II Kgs.7:3-16). No incident recorded in the Old Testament is without significance. There is in each and every one the traces of God's hand, working for His people's good and His own glory, though He be not mentioned by name. What He permitted, what He did and what it was leading to were seldom evident at the time, but when resting in the enjoyment of what He had prepared for them, His people were able to trace a chain of apparently unrelated, irksome or unpleasant happenings which led to their felicity. These things were written for our learning. Always it is of our God, the unchanging, unchangeable God that we read; always it is our situation that confronts us in Holy Writ. The conduct and experience are our own or that of relatives, friends or fellow Christians or those who would oppose and hinder our faith; and the outcome, including the commendations, rewards, chastisements or visitations of wrath are what we can anticipate. That, among other things, is what we mean by the infallible and enduring qualities of the word of God; that is what is meant by the importance and pertinence of faith. When the historical and biographical sections of the Old Testament are studied carefully, their truths build within the church's and the individual Christian's spiritual consciousness the unshakeable conviction that, however strange and painful the way, the Lord is leading us on surely to our "latter end and hope" (Jer.29:11). That is the message of the Book of Esther. As we attempt to consider it as an illustration of God's Providence at work, we will be reminded of what the Lord requires of us as we pass through the changing scenes of life, and taught that the Lord never leaves us nor forsakes us. This will permit us to say boldly, "The Lord is our helper, and we will not fear what man (and life) shall do unto us" (Heb.13:5,6).

ACCORDING TO PURPOSE

II

HE PUTTETH ONE DOWN

The form of government prevalent in Biblical times was absolute sovereignty. The king's word was law and there was no gainsaying it. He had the power of life and death, and the fate, fortune and future of his servants and subjects were in his hands entirely. Often caprice or expediency as well as political astuteness determined his promoting or demoting his officers. At one moment they could be in favour, the next in disgrace; or like Joseph, languishing in prison in the morning, a political unknown, and before nightfall, be exalted to chief officer of state because of his ability to interpret dreams.

"God is king over all the earth" (Ps.47:7) is one of the most prominent themes of Scripture. He is the monarch Who owns no equal, and concerning whose authority and power it is claimed, "The king's heart is in the hands of the Lord; he turneth it whithersoever he will" (Prov.21:1). The Lord has complete control over even the very thoughts and motives as well as the conduct of the strongest and most powerful in every land. His sovereignty is truly absolute. That is the truth which inspired the Psalmist to write, "God is judge; he putteth one down, and lifteth up another" (Ps.75:7). But how are we to understand this putting down and lifting up? We can dismiss capriciousness and expediency. The full statement found in Psalm 75, verses 4 to 8 reads, "I said unto the fools, Deal not foolishly: and to the wicked, Lift not up the horn: Lift not up your horn on high: speak not with a stiff neck. For promotion cometh neither from the east, nor from the west, nor from the south. But God is the judge: he putteth down one, and setteth up another. For in the hand of the Lord there is a cup, and the wine is red; it is full of mixture; and he poureth out the same: but the dregs thereof, all the wicked of the earth shall wring them out, and drink them". The fools and the wicked, one and the same, are those who oppose God, and the Lord is pronouncing judgment against them. Whether we translate 'rum' (v.6) to mean promotion, as we understand it, or 'to lift up' - the same word is rendered 'lift' (v.v.4,5), 'setteth up' (v.7) and 'exalted' (v.10) - there is the underlying thought of the justice of God at work; and as the Judge of all the earth, He is doing right. He puts down the wicked by cutting off their horns, thereby rendering them harmless, and so delivers the righteous from their evil designs; at the same time, the horns of the righteous are exalted, making them triumphant and secure (v.10). The evil intent directed against the people of God is an attack on His covenant; His putting down and lifting up, according to His righteous standards, is His defence of, and His securing, His covenant and people. Seen in that light, the Book of Esther is the best exposition or illustration of Psalm 75, verses 4 to 8.

Whatever financial straits historians tell us Ahasuerus was in because of his costly military campaigns, he was determined to sustain his morale and that of his people, and to impress upon his allies and subject nations that his empire was secure and prosperous. His extravagant and extended birthday celebrations were designed to achieve those ends, and to all intents and purposes succeeded. The gold and silver ornaments and dishes, the lavish draperies, the feasting and drinking, the carnival atmosphere which all, young and old, rich and poor shared, all bespoke cloudless political skies and a ridge of high pressure which would ensure the same for many years to come (Esth.1:1-9). But feasting near to the king was a man with two ambitions burning fiercely in his soul: the one, to so gain the king's favour that he would be second only to the king, if not his equal; and the other, to see a race of people, the Jews, whom he hated passionately, destroyed. He was convinced that if he could achieve the first, the second would follow as a matter of course. The man was Haman. The Book of Esther seems to infer that his intention to destroy the Jews was sparked off by Mordecai's refusal to show him worshipful respect when, having purchased some promotion, he passed to and from the palace. But such hatred and scheming and cunning as he showed against the Jews were not born and matured in a week or even months. It is possible that this hatred was inflamed by Mordecai's intelligence and integrity, features which made him a strong contender with Haman in the promotion race, and likely to succeed; and because the Jews by their commercial skills and industry had blocked some of his get-rich-quick schemes, and by their ever increasing prosperity were attracting the attention of the king as those most likely to ensure the economic stability of the state. If that were so, and it is but part of the truth, as we shall suggest later, Haman was planning and scheming and awaiting the most favourable opportunity to strike at this people. But he failed to take into account the God of the Jews, the Lord of Providence. Even while he was plotting, the God Who sees the end from the beginning had His strategy worked out, and during the feasting, when there seemed not the slightest hint of trouble, God set His counter plan in motion.

The king and his courtiers were having a great time. Man encouraged man to drink, the king fell victim to intemperance and became the slave of intoxication. The more he drank the more childish he was. The more the liquor soaked into his mind, the more uncontrolled his thoughts and tongue. The more the convivial spirit possessed him, the more he made verbal parade of his greatness and possessions. He boasted of his skill-at-arms, of the military genius which had won for him an empire; crowed about the god-like worship the people accorded him; drooled over the beauty that was his harem. That led him to become hysterically lyrical about the love and light of his life, Vashti, and he demanded that she be summoned that all might sample her beauty. The God of Providence had made His first move (Esth.1:10,11).

Vashti refused the king's request. We pass over the heavy silence which greeted her decision, and then broken by the thunderous rage of her drunken spouse. The unseen Vashti has the spotlight, and most probably that was what she intended. If she was the Amestris of secular history, as many historians believe, she was a woman

18

with a mind and temper of her own. It was she who mutilated the mother of one of the king's mistresses in a fit of jealous rage, when accompanying him on a campaign to Greece. This nearly started a revolution, but she was unrepentant. No woman would supplant her, if she could prevent it. Further, according to Herodotus, and as may be gathered from the above, she was a cruel, unscrupulous character who completely dominated her husband. In that case, her action may be seen as a way of publicly displaying her contempt for him, and of expressing the anger and scorn with which she rejected his command. She was a woman and would be treated with the respect due to her sex. She was a queen and would conduct herself as one. Not for her to stand and be gaped at by a mob of drunken, insensitive courtiers. If and when she stood before the court, it would be at her sober husband's and king's side, as his lawful consort, to assist him in his royal work and to receive with him the homage of the people in a manner befitting their rank. There is much in that which is commendable, but the remainder forbids that we show her too much charity or that we see her action as one of simple outrage.

Her forthright refusal had a sobering effect on the king and his court. Their masculine pride was punctured. She had had the temerity to expose their boorishness, to rebuff their obscenity, and to make them a laughing stock in the sight of the empire. But instead of taking her refusal to heart, apologising for the embarrassment that had been caused her, and giving an assurance that there would be no repetition of the unseemly incident, they thirsted for revenge. In the light of the previous paragraph, we can well imagine that they considered that she had gone too far this time, and that the hour had struck when she must be put in her place once for all. On the one hand, the king, still smarting from the humiliation of the Greek incident, already mentioned, and the serious breach in diplomatic relations it had caused, and fed up with her tantrums, independence and bias toward trouble making, decided he would be better off without her, particularly as he had the backing of his closest advisers. They, on the other hand, knew their womenfolk, and knowing how the queen dominated the king, were apprehensive of their own domestic authority and bliss. If her action were allowed to go unpunished, when it became public knowledge, as it would sooner or later, her conduct was likely to prove contagious. They would not be masters in their own homes. Therefore, particularly as the king was as insulted and agrieved as themselves, they took the liberty of insisting that for the peace of the realm she must be dealt with severely. Vashti must go. All were agreed, and without taking time for further reflection, divorce proceedings were put into operation and completed with indecent haste. Vashti was deposed (Esth.1:13-22). The God Who controls all events had made His second move.

But is that not an unfair assessment? Given that the Westminster Confession's doctrine of Providence is Biblical, is God's righteousness and love not called into question by Vashti's divorce? Many consider that her action was one of moral courage, in many sermons she has been set up as an example of female modesty, one who should be applauded and honoured, not dismissed to the anonymity of a Persian harem.

That sounds reasonable, particularly, if, having only the Word of God in our hands, we find ourselves confronted with a scarcity of detail. Only one incident from Vashti's life is given, and that without comment. The sacred historian is not concerned with Vashti but with how Esther came to the throne. However, no matter how Vashti's action is viewed, what befell her in the Providence of God in no way does despite to His righteousness, justice and truth.

The holy and righteous God is in no way responsible for the cruel, barbaric treatment humans dole out to each other. The mystery of Providence is that, while the Lord determines how men and nations will work and what they will do, yet whatever guilt and condemnation accompanies their actions they cannot be laid at the door of God. A closer look at the word 'determine' might help us to understand what sounds so much like fatalism. It is not a case of God saying, "You will do this or that in a particular way at a particular time and place", and there being no escape from the order. On the contrary, God cannot issue any instruction which would contravene any part of His own law. He knows the end from the beginning, knows what He has planned and purposed for His people, has fixed conclusively and authoritatively the attainment of what He has planned. It shall be achieved. That is what it is to determine. Also, He knows the fallen men and women with whom He has to do; discerns the thoughts and intents of every heart (Heb.4:12), knows how every person will act or react in a given situation, whether created by man or not, yet does nothing to prevent the situation arising or individuals behaving as they do. He allows events to take their course, but never permits them to get out of His control. Always, He imposes a limit to the evil men do, though they themselves are unaware of it. This He does by placing events and circumstances, seemingly not related, into juxtapostion with each other, the one reacting on the other in a manner He knows it will, and that to produce or contribute to the end He has ordained. That, again, is to determine. This the Lord is doing continuously, and no individual, event or circumstance, natural or manmade, is excluded. This is the mystery and glory of God's omnipresence, omniscience and omnipotence creating what we call His Providence.

That fits in with man's conception of himself and his conduct. He knows himself to be a free agent, having liberty to do more or less as he pleases, but a freedom which does not rob him of his sense of responsibility and accountablity to others. That at birth he was brought forth in iniquity (Ps.21:5), that is, born an inheritor of original sin, and that this handicap and his inability to overcome it has perverted his freedom into an evil one, one used contrary to the manner in which his Creator intended, does not lessen his responsibility and accountability one whit. He knows himself to be responsible for every breach of the law of God and of man he commits. The more he attempts to excuse his conduct and to wriggle out of facing its consequences, the more he is acknowledging that he is culpably guilty. The drunken driver who has caused the death of a pedestrian may excuse himself by saying, "I was intoxicated; I could not help myself;" but it is a plea which adds to the enormity of the crime. He should not have been drunk; he made himself so. Therefore, he must accept the consequences of his misdemeanours. None of us sees anything strange in that, nor do we consider the courts unrighteous or indifferent to the man's state, when sentencing him to his just desserts. Why, then, should there be an outcry against God, when Vashti and those like her are dealt with according to the custom and laws of the time? True, they might be dealt with harshly or inhumanely, but that is not God but man exerting his perverted freedom. In fact, Vashti could consider herself fortunate that no worse punishment befell her than being relegated to a back seat among the lesser and ex-favourites of the king. Some had lost their heads for offences more trivial than hers. Was not the Providence of God at work using whatever affection the king had left for Vashti preventing a capital sentence being carried out on her? Be that as it may, the incident is recorded as an instance of God putting down one that He might promote another whom He can use to safeguard His covenant. If, so doing, the innocent suffer, the guilt is theirs whose crimes occasioned the relegation and the promotion.

Two examples of this may be drawn from the Scriptures. The first is from the New Testament. King Herod martyred the apostle James, brother of John. It was an action which pleased the Jewish hierarchy, and that he might continue in their good graces the king, had Peter arrested, intending that he should follow James when the Passover celebrations were ended. The church prayed, but did not see how their prayers could be answered, for Peter was in the heart of the city's prison, chained between two guards, and with more guards outside his locked cell door. The Lord intervened directly. An angel possessed of supernatural powers engineered Peter's escape in such miraculous and silent fashion that none, not even the two to whom Peter was manacled, was aware of it until they awoke in the morning to prepare for the execution. Herod had all the guard questioned and, understandably, found their answers far from convincing. He ordered them to be executed for dereliction of duty. They were innocent. There was no way they could have known of, or prevented the escape; yet they suffered death. Their blood was not on the Lord's hands but on Herod's, already stained with the blood of James and itching to be further dyed in the blood of Peter. A catalogue of crimes was against the king's name. He was a murderer and a would-be murderer, he was scheming to be a church wrecker and destroyer of the covenant of grace, and in his egotism considered himself the equal of deity. These were the crimes which led to his execution of the guard. The Lord, intervening because He had further work for His servant to do, and that His church and gospel might be preserved and advanced, required, because He knew what Herod was, that the guard be put down that His apostle might be liberated. The criminality of the king was responsible from first to last, and how swiftly and fearfully the judgment of God finally overtook him. The outcome? "The word of the Lord grew and multiplied" (Acts 12:1-10, 18-24). The second incident comes from the Old Testament. A fearful blot on the life of David was his adultery with Bathsheba, followed by his outrageous murder of her husband, Uriah. Not by any stretch of the imagination can these evils be condoned. The Lord strongly condemned them, yet they led to the birth of Solomon. He was the most resplendent of Israel's kings, the one through whom the line of David, which culminated in the birth of the Messiah, was continued (II Sam.11). That was according to purpose, for the Lord Who had promised that the seed of the woman, Christ, would come and undo the work of the fall (Gen.3:15; Gal.4:4,5), chose Solomon to be his father's successor (II Sam.12:24; I Chron.22:6-10). Once again we see the Lord putting down one and lifting up another. He put down Uriah that Solomon might be; He set aside the other sons of David, some of whom considered themselves to be the rightful heirs, that Solomon might be exalted to the throne and have his place in the genealogy of Christ, that the Lord's sure mercies to David might find expression in Jesus of Nazareth, the Son of the Virgin. Yet who can doubt the righteous anger of God or the severity of the chastisements He inflicted on David (II Sam.12:19-24).

Mystery? Undoubtedly, but if God is, is eternal, dwells in light which no man can approach, that is, is unscrutable, as the Bible claims - and can He be less and be God? - mortal finite minds cannot comprehend His ways. According to the Scriptures, this God, the God of the Patriarchs, the God of the Prophets, the God and Father of our Lord Jesus Christ, is great and of great power, and His understanding is infinite. There is no searching of it (Ps.147:5; Isa.40:28). His thoughts are not our thoughts, His ways not our ways (Isa.25:8). If there is no mystery, there is no such God, and, consequently, no Providence. Providence is simply God's foresight planning, preparing, supplying, controlling, guiding, and directing all men and their affairs in order to care for and bring those who trust Him to His purposed end for them. If there is no such wise, loving, all powerful care, there is only chance, and chance includes mischance and bad luck. Chance is concerned only with the present and is most uncertain. Today's mishaps may cancel out yesterday's good fortune, may send one reeling back, who was striding forward prosperously, erasing all gain, and leaving him hurt, bewildered and bereft of confidence. Few there are, if any, who, accepting chance as the ruling factor in their lives, can escape the conclusion that their lives have as much prospect of a sure and safe end, as has a leaking, rudderless boat adrift on an ocean alternating between storm and calm. Where there is no Providence there is no faith, indeed, there is no place for faith. Faith is the confidence that unseen Love and Good are working ceaselessly, though perhaps not apparently, on one's behalf, and that whatever the event, circumstance or experience, whether it be what others call setback, hindrance or even defeat, is contributing to one's advance toward the goal Love has ordained. Providence is design, chance is chaos; and without faith's recognition of God's ways and dealings, there can be no hope for men caught in the tangled skein of human life. To view with hindsight all the way that God has led the believer, to see the hand of the Lord in the history of the Church, her story being worked out according to Bible prophecy and teaching, to trace the sequence of events in the biographies and autobiographies of the saints of God, is to have before us, as it were, a canvas filled with a mass of colours, which like many modern abstract paintings, seem not to make much sense. But having some understanding of God's style, and knowing He is the artist, the more the design and art form are contemplated, the more clear the Artist's intent and, often, the more breath-taking its imagination, scope and beauty. As we view, we find ourselves saying with Paul, "O the depth of the riches both of the wisdom and knowledge of God! how unsearchable his judgements, and his ways past finding out!" (Rom.11:33).

While the foregoing gives some appreciation of God's wisdom and power, it still poses the question in many minds, "Does it give Him the right to put down one that he might raise up or promote another?" The understanding of so-called human rights prevalent today leads many to answer in the negative. For them, human or civil rights is freedom from all restraint and discipline. This immoral philosophy is responsible for more disruptions of everyday life than possibly any other factor. The right of those in positions of authority to place, unplace or replace others is an essential feature of a well ordered, prosperous society. In industry, if a manager is known to be inefficient, the board of directors has the right to either dismiss him or transfer him to another department where he is likely to prove more useful; in cricket, if the captain of the test team is not winning matches, the selectors soon replace him with another whom they hope will prove more successful. In both cases, the men concerned are not doing the job expected of them, and since success and prosperity are vital, it becomes imperative to remove them. If they are not, there is an outcry from those who suffer most from the incompetence and failure to rectify the situation, and the protesting persists until the matter is put right. If this putting down and setting up is esential to the affairs of this life and is insisted on by men, has God not the same right when prosecuting His affairs? He too must have the right person in the right place at the right time. There is an important difference, however. Boards and committees remove men because they have proved unequal to their tasks; God often removes them before they prove incapable of doing what He wants. He knows what will be required of the occupant of a post in the not too distant future, and if the present incumbent is not what is required, he is removed before any harm can be done and replaced by the right person. According to the will of God, Vashti was deposed, not because she had proved herself a poor queen or an unfaithful or incompetent wife, but because by no stretch of the imagination could she be seen defending the Jews. The impending fate of those exiles would not have prostrated her with grief, would not have moved her to call the Jews and her entourage to fast that they might pray for Israel's deliverance, or made her willing to be prepared to sacrifice her all that she might intercede with the king on their behalf, or adopt womanly cunning that that intercession might be effective. But Esther could and would do all that. She herself was a Jewess, possessed with the faith and courage of her fathers. That was why Vashti was replaced.

But there is a more fundamental reason why God has the right to depose and promote as He sees fit, namely, His right as Creator of all. All is His. "He has created all things, and for his pleasure they are and were created" (Rev.4:11). He was under no compulsion from any quarter to create. He did so according to the good pleasure of His own will and for His own satisfaction. Therefore, His is the right of ownership to make, to place, to remove, direct and control that that satisfaction might be attained. Paul likens individuals to clay in the hands of a potter. From the same lump of clay he makes an object of rare distinction and an ordinary pot of common shape, without beauty, to be used for the most menial of purposes. No one quarrels with that, least of all the clay; neither, argues the apostle, should we quarrel with the Creator's right to make and place and use us as He pleases (Rom.9:20,21), particularly, as He does so to demonstrate the glory of His holiness and the riches of His grace (Rom.9:22,23). That view many object to. They are not inanimate lumps of clay but human beings, full of life and vitality, with reason and emotions and will. It is degrading to talk of them being manipulated into being and doing what they do not choose. Popular as such a view is, it does not square with the facts. We are all creatures of the dust, formed by God alone (Ps.139:14-16) and for Himself alone. We were brought into this world without being consulted; we possess features, faculties, talents and a leaning toward particular habits and employments that were none of our choosing. They were transmitted to us through our parents at conception, the transmitting agent being the Spirit of God, from Whom all life proceeds. What we are we did not request, nor could we make protest against it. We are as God made us, sin excepted, and have been brought into this world as instruments of His good pleasure. Men might boast of their independence, freedom and achievements, as though each were self-made, a small self-sufficient island in the great human archipelago set in the vast ocean of the universe; but Paul in typical fashion cuts all such down to size when he says, "Who maketh thee to differ from another? and what hast thou that thou didst not receive? now, if thou didst receive it, why dost thou glory as if thou hadst not received it?" (I Cor.4:7). Whether an individual knows God, acknowledges Him or dismisses Him as a fiction, God is his maker, has made him what he is, has placed him in this world and is using him. That is God the Creator's prerogative which He has never surrendered to any.

But, despite what was said earlier, does that not make God the author of sin? Paul does say, "Whom (God) will he hardeneth" (Rom.9:18). That is to ignore the context and the incidents of Moses' conflict with Pharaoh recorded in Exodus. There we read that when God sent Moses to demand from the king the release of the Jews, He warned him, "I am sure that the king of Egypt will not let you go, no, not by a mighty hand" (Ex.3:19). God knew through and through this king with whom He was dealing. Pharaoh was a man of a hard heart who, despite all that he saw of the power of God, deliberately made his heart harder (Ex.8:15,32; 9:34). Of course, it does say repeatedly that God hardened Pharaoh's heart (Ex.4:21; 7:3; 8:15; 9:12; 10:20,27; 14:4,8,17). He did so, simply by with-holding His mercy from one who had no desire for it. Paul writes, "It is not of him that willeth, nor of him that runneth, but of God that sheweth mercy" (Rom.9:16). God knew what Pharaoh was, and said, "For this cause have I raised thee up, for to shew thee my power; and that my name may be glorified throughout all the earth'' (Ex.9:16; Rom.9:17). God, without Whom Pharaoh could not be born, permitted his birth and upbringing, and simply used what he was, without being responsible for it. Michelangelo, the XVIth Century sculptor, when visiting a quarry, saw a block of marble with a huge curve cut into one side. Enquiring why, he was informed that a would be sculptor had purchased the block, inexpertly cut the curve, and then found that he could do nothing more with it. Michelangelo ordered the slab to be delivered to his studio. In the course of time there was unveiled one of his great masterpieces, David leaning back, poised to hurl a sling stone at Goliath's head. The master used the incompetence of another to his own advantage. The Lord God is no less skilful in his use of men, together with their flaws, weaknesses and sins. He used Ahasuerus's drunken pride to put Esther in the place of greatest influence against the day when that position would be vital to His people, the Jews. Had it been a man, and not God, that did that, it would have been heralded as a stroke of genius. He used the butler's forgetfulness to keep Joseph in prison until He had prepared a place for him at Pharaoh's right hand. He used the insane pride of Nebuchadnezzar and the inveterate jealousy of his courtiers to have Daniel's three friends cast into an overheated furnace because they would not compromise their faith by worshipping an idol. Why? To prove to Nebuchadnezzar and his court that all the gods of Babylon and its subject territories were nothing but grotesque figments of a depraved imagination, that the God of Shadrach, Meshach and Abednego is the living God, the protector and sustainer of His people, though they be in a foreign land, and He alone must be worshipped by all peoples (Dan.3).

He putteth down one. Perhaps the deposing and divorcing of Vashti caused a sensation in the kingdom, or maybe it was nothing more than a nine days wonder, gossip soon to be replaced by other items of news or scandal, and she forgotten. At that time the event had no political significance, the nation carried on as though nothing had happened. But God had worked and God waited. When the crisis came and went, few, if any, in the kingdom had any thought for Vashti or paused to consider that she had had an unsought, passive role in the triumph of the Jews. Her dismissal was nothing more than a fact recorded in the Chronicles of State and unread by the vast majority. Mordecai, Esther and other folks of faith in the light of what transpired understood the connection, and the incident was recorded in the scripture of truth for the comfort and encouragement of the church and people of God. The message of Vashti's fate is: events are taking place all around us which seem to have no reference to the grace purposes of God or significance for the church, are not considered to be too important and are soon forgotten. But all the mass of happenings is under the watchful eye of Him Who sees the end from the beginning, is not outwith His control and purpose. Always, He is positioned to act positively when the need arises. We need not fear the unexpected crises which arise occasionally and threaten the peace of Christians and the church. The Lord knew it was coming, had His instruments ready for operation, has cleared the way for action and, providing we play our part as we should, there need be no despair. The outcome is sure.

ACCORDING TO PURPOSE
III
HE SETS ANOTHER UP

"The Lord knows the secrets of the heart" (Ps.44:21), of every heart. He made the heart. He knows it moods and longings, its desires and ambitions, its emptiness and with what man would fill it. He knows also how man responds to life in order that that emptiness might be satisfied, and secretly and skillfully He brings empty hearts into conjunction with each other, gratifying their urges and so furthers His own designs. That briefly is the story of Esther chapter 2.

Ahasuerus was a king with an empty heart. Vashti had meant more to him than he knew. Sobriety, remembrance and loneliness brought home to him what he had drunkenly and stupidly surrendered. His remorse was painful in the extreme, made more so by the knowledge that her divorce was absolute. Or was it? His councillors understanding his uncertain temper and vacillations saw the possibility of him repealing the decree and taking her back. That could not be tolerated. Not only would it condone Vashti's conduct, give her carte blanche to behave as she liked in the future and so encourage discontent and revolution in their own harems, a possibility her divorce was intended to prevent, but it would destroy the foundation of the legal system of the Medes and Persians. This ordained that no royal decree could be altered or removed from the statute book. Were that to happen, the State would be ungovernable; so they urgently advised the king to set in motion the procedures for appointing a new wife and queen.

Mordecai was a man with an empty chamber in his heart, a room which must be filled with the satisfaction of advancement at court for himself and the security of his ward, Esther. These account for his determination to keep his own and his niece's national identity secret. Esther chapter 3, verse 4 suggests that his associates were unaware he was a Jew until he was forced to give the reason why he refused to make obeisance before Haman, and that there was an under-current of antisemitism in the State likely to prove a barrier to favour and promotion. These two empty hearts, Ahasuerus' and Mordecai's, were to derive satisfaction from the recommendation of the king's cabinet. The God Whose hand none can stay had made His third move.

The king consented to the organising of the equivalent of the modern 'Miss World' contest. Whatever else she might be the king's consort must be pleasing to the eye, if not the most beautiful in the land. Consequently, the organisers were detailed to scour the land and to conscript the fairest virgins and prepare them for the scrutiny and approval or otherwise of the king. The time of preparation was long and costly, each girl having the right, at the king's expense, to display her beauty to the best advantage in her bid to win the monarch's heart. The prize was a glittering one, elevation to the throne and acknowledged first lady of the land, but the stakes were high and there was no backing out. It was a case of the winner taking all and the losers losing all. They whom the king rejected were relegated to the well nigh forgotten, sealed off feminine quarters of an eastern potentate's palace, probably never to be seen or heard of again. The youthful Esther found herself an unwilling participant in the contest. From her entrance into the palace and throughout the year long course of training and beauty treatment she was the favourite of Hegei, the eunuch responsible for the welfare of the girls concerned. What was it that attracted Esther to him? We can rule out bribery; to such corrupt practice a man of Mordecai's righteous calibre would not stoop, though doubtless many of the girls' parents would make money talk in an attempt to advantage their daughters. Nor can we imagine that Esther's social standing was sufficiently high to automatically merit the preferential treatment she received. Nurtured in a faith and culture and environment alien to what she now found herself in, perhaps it was her demureness, her modesty and shyness which gave added depth to her beauty, causing her to stand out from the rest, which won Hegei's heart and caused him intuitively to know that she was the girl for the king. We do not know; but of this we can be sure, it was the Lord Who had given and used the secondary means that made her Hegei's choice. Joseph is the precedent which leads to that conclusion. There was a winsomeness in his personality which attracted others to him as a magnet does steel. This charisma the sacred record describes as the presence of the Lord (Gen.39:3). Potiphar saw this presence in the lad's transparent honesty and his intelligent handling of any task entrusted to him, and so gave him more and more responsibility until he became chief steward of the household. This presence, honesty and intelligence did not forsake him in prison, nor did he forsake them. There we find him singled out for special duties by the prison governor. The Lord gave Joseph favour in the eyes of those who mattered, favour which led to the necessary preparation for what God had in mind. The same was true of Daniel and his three friends, numbered among the prisoners of war Nebuchadnezzar had earmarked for special service at court. They won the heart of the principal eunuch responsible for their education (Dan.1:9). Here, however, the four friends used the favouritism to secure permission to forego the luxurious living standards accorded to students, and to partake of a spartan diet more in keeping with their determination to keep themselves unspotted from the world and more conducive to the health and alertness of both body and mind. By this favouritism God kept them apart from the other students and equipped them for what the future held in store. Esther is included in this goodly company. She was favoured by the world that she might be made ready for what had been made ready for her. In each case it was the Lord's doing, and marvellous in their eyes and ours.

It must not be overlooked, however, that though each of the above was favoured, their circumstances cannot be described as favourable in human terms. Left to themselves each would have preferred being elsewhere. Joseph was debased as a bondservant and as a convict unjustly condemned. Daniel and his three friends were forced into a pagan environment which was slowly but irrevocably sapping the moral and physical vitality of those creating and revelling in it. The four Jews had to live in it as the odd men out; never an easy, pleasant or comfortable position. Esther was passive in an atmosphere which was alien to her and subject to the dictates of her guardian, and her future, whichever way it went, was scarcely attractive to her. Each was promoted by the Lord for the work He had for them to do; each was brought to that promotion by the favouritism of the world, and in a sense each of them earned that promotion by being what they were as the children of God. The favour of the world is a blessing from God when it is neither expected nor worked for, when it is not gained by obsequious conduct - the child of God must never grovel before the world for any of its prizes - and when it comes because one's light is shining before men and seen in good works by which they glorify their Father in heaven. Each of the characters dealt with was humble, content, co-operative and competent, sought no reward from the world, was convinced that the Lord had chosen his or her lot and that whatever the outcome, faithfulness to God and righteousness were their first priority. All the rest was left with God and He was ever at hand to bless. The Lord was with them and they prospered. The Lord was with them to promote for His glory.

Who were these individuals? What was their secret? We link them together because they had so much in common, much which is vital to the Lord's purpose in every age, much that is characteristic of those whom the Lord promotes. Before discussing this we must first consider what promotion means.

Our understanding of promotion is advancement in one's chosen vocation or career, and the elevation of the three under review may be seen in that light. But when the Psalmist speaks of promotion, he means setting up, God putting an individual in a position where he can be used as God pleases. That gives a grey, if not a black, side to promotion which is not always palatable to the recipient. When Joseph was sold as a slave, when he was maliciously accused of indecency by Potiphar's wife and condemned on her evidence, when he was forgotten by Pharaoh's butler and left to languish in gaol, on each of these occasions he was promoted according to God's use of the term. To our way of thinking, he was being pushed down until he could scarcely reach a lower level, but in reality he was where God had set him up. The same is true also of Esther. Assuming she was born in exile, she would not be very old before she learned that exile was the most awful humiliation which could be inflicted on her people and on herself as a Jewess. Her parents died, and calamity was piled upon calamity, forcing her down to lower mournful levels. Worse was to come. It seemed to her that she had hit the bottom of the abyss when conscripted as a candidate for the affection and favours of a pagan king. That was the final disgrace. She felt as though her beauty, her virtue, her modesty and her faith were being prostituted. The wrath of God was upon her; she saw herself included in the fearful curse, "Thy daughters shall be given to another people" (Deut.28:32). In her estimation she could sink no deeper, but that was where the Lord set her up. How Daniel loathed the education he was receiving in Babylon's chief university, riddled as it was with the superstitions and the conjectures of darkened minds abhorrent to any instructed in the counsel of God and enjoying the liberty it gives. How soiled and contaminated his mind seemed; could a scholar be more degraded! God had set him up. The Lord Whose thoughts and ways are as high above ours as the heavens are above the earth, often sets His children on the refuse heaps of life. There He will use them. That is their promotion.

This setting up is an honour and a privilege. They have been chosen to it by the Lord of glory for the successful execution of His business. A doubtful honour? Certainly not! For what is an individual apart from the grace of God? The fairest and the most talented and skilful of the sons of men is but the broken down ruin of Adam, and his utopias and shang-le-rais the figments of a fevered imagination or like the fantasies of surrealist artists. When the grace of God lays hold on any such - and none is exempt from this ruin - to save and restore, to train and equip for the work of the kingdom of heaven, the refuse heap, the lowest and meanest place where He intends to use one must be considered promotion. It is infinitely higher than can be expected, deserved or personally attained. The extent of this privilege may be viewed from another angle. When God in His mercy put into operation the work of salvaging and redeeming individuals for Himself and His service, He chose as His workman the only Son of His love. That Son, His only begotten Son, could not by native right be higher in glory and honour; for He was in the form of God (Philp.2:6), the one Whom God has appointed the heir of all things, Who is the brightness of God's glory, the express image of His person, the co-occupant of the thrones of heaven and the universe (Heb.1:2,3). This choice necessitated His Son becoming incarnate as man, so veiling His original nature that none recognised Him as the Lord of glory. As man, a peasant, a labourer, an itinerant preacher despised by the Jewish hierarchy, he submitted to being made sin for sinners, despite His proven impeccable holiness and righteousness, descending into the lowest hell and into death in order to effect their redemption. It is impossible to exaggerate or understand how low He stooped, yet He considered the appointment promotion. Speaking by His Spirit through the Psalmist, the Son tells us how He regarded His commission: "Lo, I come," He said, "in the volume of the book it is written of me, I delight to do thy will, O my God; yea, thy law is within my heart" (Ps.40:7,8). He regarded His incarnation and the consequences which flowed from it as a supreme honour. His Father had chosen and set Him up as the Saviour of the world. The Lord is promoting even when He sets up low, but the lower He sets the higher He exalts ultimately. None was set lower than His Son, but the Son, being obedient, was highly exalted and given a name which is above every name, one before which every knee must bow, of things in heaven and things on earth, and things under the earth, and every tongue confess Him Lord to the glory of God the Father (Philp.2:9-11). The trio on whose histories we have been concentrating also experienced the exalting power of God, as did the Virgin Mary whose mysterious pregnancy made her suspect in the eyes of her betrothed and, no doubt, of many others beside. She was set up low, and then lifted up to be "highly favoured, blessed among women" (Lk.1:28). These are but samples of the many gleaned from the Scripture narrative whom the Lord promoted. He has not changed His method of operation.

Returning to what our heroine and two heroes had in common: first, each of them was promoted within the secular sphere to a secular position. By secular is meant that which belongs to the world and time and is temporal, as distinct from that which is spiritual and eternal. Many confuse the secular with the worldliness which is spoken against everywhere in the New Testament, but they are not identical. Worldliness is the shroud which clothes those who are dead in trespasses and sins, the comfort they seek from the ephemeral in this life, being lovers of pleasure more than lovers of God, and fondly imagining that life consists of what is possessed and that they live by bread alone. Unfortunately, it is a garment which many Christians covet and have taken to themselves. Worldliness in the Christian is a spirit of self-gratification which places an undue emphasis on what appertains to this life, relegates God, His kingdom and righteousness to second or even a lower place in their scheme of things. We must beware of the leaven of the Pharisees. The Pharisee was an eminently religious man, considered himself spiritual, but was the epitome of worldliness. That is what the New Testament would have Christians guard against by exhorting us to daily present our bodies to Christ as living sacrifices, holy, acceptable to God, and as our reasonable service (Rom.12:1). Whereas, the secular is the creation in which we find ourselves, of which we are part, and all of which should be used for man's physical and temporal welfare. Paul teaches that "every creature (provision) of God is good, and nothing to be refused, if it be received with thanksgiving; for it is sanctified by the word of God and prayer" (I Tim.4:4). The secular is the natural sphere of man. Its ordinances of government were ordained by God for his good. Its delights and benefits, and the talents, skills and abilities the means by which we may legitimately, constructively and profitably partake of them. All is the gift of God, and man's responsible use of it the service he renders to his fellows and to God. If man as we now know him makes all that seem unreal, it nevertheless remains true and is what should be. The Christian, as much as in him lies, must make it so. The secular is the realm in which he lives and moves, works and plays, serves and is served, rules or is ruled. It is also the theatre in which God is working His purposes out and where His people are co-workers together with Him.

The dividing of the Christian's life into the secular and the spiritual is an unhappy, unnatural one. It makes for a negative attitude toward life which encourages the spirit of worldliness dealt with above. It prevents many finding job satisfaction and glorifying God in their appointed place, causeing them to forego, and that to their detriment, what the Lord has provided for their recreation. But more importantly, it fails to take into account the importance of the secular to God. He Himself has given it this importance. All the epoch making events of the kingdom of God on earth took place within the secular realm and by secular means, and that includes both the exodus from Egypt and the crucifixion of Christ. And it is the theatre of service to which He sends the vast majority of His servants. When the story of the Church is unfolded in heaven, then will it be known that all of her outstanding advances were made in this zone. An objection to all that might be that the secular is under the control or domination of him whom Jesus called "the prince of this world". Without doubt, this person by his manipulation of fallen man has degraded the world to a state of worldliness, considers it his own and which he uses to make war on Christ and His grace and kingdom. That was true when Joseph, Daniel and Esther were alive, and their histories declare that God has not surrendered His sovereignty to Satan, that this is still God's world, and that His people can still obtain the utmost good from it and be most useful to the Lord in it. The saints of old lived and worked in societies which could not have been more godless, they seemed to be a minority of one or a little more, but that was their strength. The communities in which they worked were bent on the destruction of the kingdom of God. They were doing work, often the most servile in character, beneficial to those communities, and because co-operating and causing little or no harm, were not considered a threat to the status quo or the aspirations of the state. In reality, these servants of God were infiltrators into enemy lines, acting as double agents, doing work important to their earthly masters, yet being used by God to pull down the strongholds of evil and to contribute to the victory of the kingdom of heaven. This is a truth being forced upon the Church today. Alarmed by the decline in church attendance and the like, some sections of the Church have recruited and trained worker-priests and placed them in factories and other hives of industry. While we would pray for their success, we cannot escape the conviction that their workmates, having little or no desire for the Christian Faith, will in the main spurn their advances. It is as though a general dropped some soldiers into enemy territory with placards bearing the caption, "We are spies come to destroy your present way of life." Every Christian in his field of labour is a worker-priest and his working clothes are his priestly garments. He should conduct himself as such by diligent, loyal labour, ever careful to keep himself unspotted from the worldliness with which he is surrounded, ever ready to give to any who enquire a reason for his separation, and ever prepared to seize every opportunity to do good to all men. By this testimony and conduct will the seed of truth be sown and hearts wooed to Christ. Similarly, many emerging countries and nations with deep rooted religions of their own, fearing the power of the gospel have banned Christian missionaries. They are prepared to take teachers, medical personnel and engineers, individuals who will improve the educational, health and economic standards of the country. What an excellent opportunity this is for Christians to infiltrate heathenism with the gospel and by means of a purer morality, consecrated labour and the ability to love one's neighbour as oneself directly influence for Christ those whom they teach, nurse or work with. This was the secret of the Church's rapid success in the earliest days of her witness; opportunity is being given today for history to repeat itself.

Another feature our trio had in common is that they were educated or trained within the secular sphere for the work the Lord had prepared for them. This goes without saying. Specialist work requires the requisite preparation. Was Joseph destined to be Egypt's minister of supply? He must be taught the skills of accountancy, of sound investment, judicious trading, of harbouring resources and distribution; and he had no better school than Potiphar's house and estate, where he had his introduction to Egyptian business methods, and where his apprenticeship was served not only in theory but in practice. Moses, for whom was reserved the onerous offices of military commander of, and statesman to, twelve enslaved and quarrelsome tribes, to weld them into a nation, a task which made him the loneliest of men, can be included in our group. He was equipped for his life's work by what the universities and military academies of Egypt could teach him and then by the solitary, sacrifical existence of a shepherd. Daniel who would rise to be the most polished politician in Babylon learned his political philosophy at the feet of Chaldean experts. Esther, in common with all Jewish maidens, learned domestic skills in the home of her guardian and, since it is probable that Mordecai was either a bachelor or a widower, something of the responsibilities of a queen as the female head of his household. There is no need to emphasize the correctness of this. In order to be efficient and responsible in business and to make a profitable contribution to a healthy, contented home and community one must submit to the discipline of training. What gives added significance to the Christian's secular education is that unknown to him the Lord might be qualifying him for work of importance with reference to the kingdom of heaven. This should make the weariness of study, the sacrifice of leisure and of little income purposeful, particularly in a day of high unemployment when the end product of a concentrated period of study might be, as far as one can judge, nothing more than a diploma or a third rate or dead end job. The Lord requires the right training for His work, and He is the best judge of what that is. To accept that whatever our academic pursuit or job, the Lord is the director of our studies, the professor in whose faculty we are being instructed, the instructor who patiently teaches line upon line, precept upon precept, and who painstakingly leads from subject to subject until He has completed that which concerns His trainees and they are ready to graduate to what He has planned, gives a meaning and dignity to the most mundane life which no earthly honour can match. This course of study might involve the discipline of unsettlement. As with the fermenting of good wine, the Lord does not permit His students to rest upon their lees. Such a settlement is destructive. It means a thickening or curding which makes the wine useless, fit only for throwing out (cf.Zeph.1:12). For Joseph or Esther, settled comfortably in their father's or guardian's home, favoured and petted, the outlook was pleasing, prosperous, desirable, but uneventful and purposeless. Sudden squalls blew providentially and there was a rude awakening for one in the house of an Egyptian and for the other in the women's quarters of a king's palace. Even there, however poor a substitute for what had been, human nature being what it is, those concerned soon settled down to a pleasant enough routine. It was comparatively easy to make the best of a bad job, conditions warranted no complaint; but when one was beginning to think that after all life was not too bad, and the other that being a queen had its compensations, once again the placid waters of their existence were disturbed. Joseph found himself in prison and Esther at the centre of a national crisis. Joseph with his flair for readjustment and disillusioned by the frailties of human nature was resigned to a lengthy, if not a life, prison sentence, and soon had an outlet for his talents and energies. But to what purpose the waste of a life incarcerated in a dungeon? The Lord could not afford that such a gem of purest ray serene should continue to inhabit a dark unfathomed cave. The king had a couple of dreams. His superstitious mind convinced him that they had to do with the affairs of state, but neither he nor his cabinet could see the connection. Then a butler remembered - once again, an angel of the Lord had troubled the waters with such force that that deep, unwholesome den was compelled to release its treasure, and it became the fairest jewel in Pharaoh's crown. Similarly with Esther: the storm of national crisis which upset her domestic routine, thrust her to the forefront of a political situation which brought her fame as the champion and deliverer of the Jews. Both were disturbed that God's covenant might not be, unsettled that what God had established in heaven might be secure on earth. The disrupting influences the Lord sends neither drown nor separate from Him but sweep one on to the pinnacle of foreordained purpose and blessing.

Another soul strengthening discipline which promotion from the Lord imposes is that of combating the jealousy of those passed over. Advancement is favour and favour is to prefer one to others. Many of those passed over feel aggrieved, knowing a hundred and one reasons why they should have been chosen. Their annoyance is vented on the promoted. This jealousy sometimes shows itself in acts of naked aggression, as witness Joseph's brothers' dealings with him, but more often than not its barb lies in its subtlety. With smoothed tongued flattery those envious of Daniel's advancement contrived to have him flung to the lions, while they masqueraded in the guise of loyal subjects concerned only for the glory of the king's majesty. The Scriptures are silent on other suggestions of jealousy against Joseph, Esther and Daniel, but it requires no great imagination to know that they felt its sting continually. Could Esther be where she was, for the purpose she was and favoured as she was and not know the spitefulness of the other women involved? From the moment favour was extended to each of our trio, they felt the venom and discomfort of lying, deceitful, slanderous whispers, of hurtful remarks, of assistance given or orders obeyed grudgingly, and of hindrances put in their way. None of it is pleasant, is not easily ignored, but should be kept in perspective by the Christian. Jealousy, being one of the besetting sins of mankind, is an occupational hazard the promoted of the Lord must expect to meet, and should be accepted as part of the Lord's package and, therefore, beneficial, if responded to in the right spirit. It encourages humility, being the reminder that there are others equally competent for the situation, that it has been given in grace and with a special end in view. So considered, determination is increased to be as proficient as one can in order to prove worthy of the trust and to ensure that the ordained end is reached. As with Joseph and Daniel, this leads to increased efficiency, opens the door to further advancement and expands the orbit of influence. To keep one's head, to do what is right, and to commit one's cause to the Lord, as did Daniel, when the green-eyed monster strikes, is to make the jealous as ineffective as the lions among whom he slept.

Perhaps the most significant feature of the three whose promotions from the Lord have had our attention is that from childhood they knew, had been instructed in, had their faith founded upon the word or revelation of the Lord. None of them could remember a time when the word of the Lord was not part of their education, was not the guide of their youth. With the Psalmist they could say, "Thou art my hope, O Lord God; thou art my trust from my youth; by thee I have been upheld from the womb" (Ps.71:5,6). In that confession there is gratitude for the godly example, instruction and counsel of parents in the Lord and of the Church, and a proved confidence in God which exerts itself in every time of need or crisis. The confidence grew out of the instruction as faith obeyed its precepts and put into practice the wisdom it inculcated and the conduct it advocated. Hiding God's word in the heart, having respect unto the ways of the Lord, and choosing the way of truth, these souls developed a strength and stability of character and trod a path of life which made them distinctive as the children of God and reliable and trustworthy in the affairs of men. They are typical of the Lord's choosing and forming of those whom He would have do His will and work.

This is a feature which should be coveted for every child in a Christian home and congregation, for its importance can scarcely be exaggerated. Almost without exception the great heroes of the Jewish Faith whose names, writings and exploits are inscribed indelibly on the pages of the Old Testament, who were brought to the kingdom of Israel to perform some outstanding feat or feats in order to preserve and advance God's covenant scheme, were brought up from infancy in the nurture and admonition of the Lord. Of each it could be said that "from childhood they had known the holy scriptures which were able to make them wise unto salvation" (II Tim.3:15). That is not to say that they and only they and their like could or can be champions of the Faith. The miracle of regeneration and conversion, which even children brought up in godliness must experience, as it came to Rahab, Ruth, Naaman, the Philippian gaoler and countless thousands more whose names and fame are registered in the annals of the Church give the lie to that. But the Scriptures never minimise the importance of the child. The instructions given to the Israelites to instill the law of God into the hearts of their children (Deut.4:9; 6:7), the resolve of the Psalmist and his contemporaries not to hide from the young the wonders of the Lord (Ps.78:4-7), the call of the wise man to parents to "train up a child in the way he should go" (Prov.22:6) and to the young to "remember now thy Creator in the days of thy youth, while the evil days come not, nor the years draw nigh, when thou shalt say, I have no pleasure in them" (Eccl.12:1) give the children a central place in the covenant not only for their own salvation's sake, but also for the good God will accomplish through them in adulthood. The emphasis is no less marked in the New Testament. From the words of Jesus, "Permit the little children to come unto me, and forbid them not, for of such is the kingdom of heaven" (Matt.10:14) to Paul's, "Fathers, bring up your children in the nurture and admonition of the Lord" (Eph.6:4) the message is clear: children are the heritage of the Lord; regard them as such, as such educate them in the truths of the Lord, direct their feet in the ways of the Church of God, equip them morally and spiritually for their predestined place in life. They might never be a Luther or a Wilberforce, a Livingstone or a Mary Slessor, but they will prove to be pillars of society, the salt of the earth, and theirs will be the epitaph Paul gave to David - and better no man can have - "after he had served his generation by the will of God, he fell asleep" (Acts 13:36). That is a testimony that can be given of the humblest labourer as well as the most notable crowned head. And one of the highest accolades which can come to a Christian parent is what the Lord said of Abraham, "I know him, that he will command his children and his household after him, and they shall keep the way of the Lord, to do justice and judgment" (Gen.18:19). It is echoed in Paul's commendation of the mother and grandmother of Timothy, "I call to remembrance the unfeigned faith that is in thee, and which dwelt first in thy grandmother Lois, and thy mother Eunice, and I am persuaded is in thee also" (II Tim.1:5). Abraham, Lois and Eunice could say from the domestic platform what the Apostle John said from the spiritual, "I have no greater joy than to hear that my children walk in the truth" (III John 4); and neither has any other Christian parent. To know the thrill of household salvation, to know that one's children have a reputation for being men and women in Christ, is the joy of knowing that the children are in the presence of the Lord at His coming, that they are the glory and joy of the parents (cf.I Thess.2:19). In other words, the parents' joy is that of the missionaries who, having gone forth with weeping bearing precious seed, are returned with rejoicing, bringing their sheaves with them (Ps.126:6). There is no more rewarding mission field than the family circle.

From such households came those whom the Lord delighted to promote in His own time and way and for His own ends. Why? We could say, and say correctly, that it was His sovereign will and be content to leave it there; but that is an evasion rather than an answer. God, exercising His sovereign will, is never arbitrary. Always there is reason, wisdom, aptness in His choices, though at the time men might not consider it so, as did David's father and brothers when the prophet called to anoint the future king of Israel. When God chooses for His work, He does so with the deliberation, determination and authority of one who knows he is not making a mistake, that He can choose no other. Further, that so many from spiritual homes, having a thorough spiritual training to which they had responded positively, were called to special service cannot be without significance. It suggests that all were possessed of a common quality and that it was this quality which most impressed those mortals responsible for their promotions in the world. This was touched upon at the beginning of the chapter, but here we want to give it one name which might be applied to each person, however individualistically each portrayed it. The quality is naturalness. There was nothing affected or artificial in the manner in which they lived. They were themselves. They were men and women of faith, but their religion did not so protrude that it was it and not they that was seen. There is nothing more off-putting than a self advertising religion which blots out the personalities of those wearing it. Esther's, Joseph's, David's was seen in the rational, intelligent conduct of their everyday lives. Their religious upbringing and their spiritual training had been so imprinted on their personalities by usage that they were able to think and act in a spiritual manner, think and act truth and righteousness, think and act the glory of God without thinking these things. That is, they thought and acted in these ways in the same manner that they breathed, without conscious effort. It was as abhorrent to Joseph to respond to the wiles of Potiphar's wife as it was for his lungs to inhale noxious fumes. Daniel could no more tolerate the luxuries of Nebuchadnezzar's court than could his healthy lungs the rarefied atmosphere of an oxygen tent. Motivated by the truth of God from infancy and from preference and by practice they were faithful to the law of righteousness and produced the fruits of righteousness. This was a fruitfulness which made them attractive and profitable to others, a beauty which being seen at its true worth in lower spheres was brought to shine in higher. Thus is it done to those whom the King of kings delights to honour. True, that is not the lot of the rank and file of the righteous of the Lord. They are strangers to the favour and the advancements gained in the world, but that does not mean that a question mark must be put against their worth. It should not be forgotten that as every organ of the human body has its rightful place and function, and that none, not even the appendix, is useless, so is it with the body of Christ. No member is out of place. Each has a definite purpose. Each is in the place of the Lord's appointment. That makes it a promotion. Ultimately, they that be wise in their appointed place shall shine as the brightness of the firmament (Dan.12:3). No other promotion can top that.

ACCORDING TO PURPOSE
IV
PROVIDENTIAL CONTRASTS

Having introduced the reader to the principals engaged in this drama, the narrative moves on to tell what the plot is and to set the scene of its unfolding. This it does from chapter 2, verse 21 through to chapter 3, verse 15. Here the author skilfully brings to our attention the chief actors, Esther excepted, in a manner which contrasts them one with the other and prepares us for the final outcome, the triumph of good over evil, of right over wrong, engineered by the unseen, unnamed Controller of events, the God of Providence.

1. Mordecai and Haman.
The stage on which the drama of the Book of Esther was enacted had its foundations in history. The hero of the book, Mordecai and the villian, Haman were the products of their respective national pasts, and the Lord Who is the God of the past as well as the present and the future was the director of the play. In common with all directors He knew what were the details of the plot, what it was meant to achieve, and how its climax could be reached satisfactorily. He knew intimately the characters with whom He was dealing and how best to motivate, control and move them, while allowing them the full and free expression of what they were. When the curtain falls on the last act, He, the players and the audience, ourselves know that the players have conducted themselves according to type, that the performance was an unforced, natural one, and that He, the director has accomplished what He set out to achieve.

Mordecai is the Lord's man, the man of faith and obedience. Though in exile, he together with his compatriots, while comfortable and prosperous, daily lamented, "If I forget thee, O Jerusalem, let my right hand forget its skills; if I do not remember thee, let my tongue cleave to the roof of my mouth; if I prefer not Jerusalem to my chiefest joy" (Ps.137:5,6). If for reasons of expediency, he choose to hide his national roots from his non-Jewish colleagues (Esth.3:4), nonetheless, he was a true patriot steeped in the religious and political lore of his people, fired with the national aspirations the promises of God inspired, and withal content, submissive to the chastisements of the Lord, confident that the Lord would arise in mercy when His set time to favour Zion had come, and Israel be restored (Ps.102:13). That was what made him what he was in exile, a law abiding citizen, concerned for the well-being of the society in which he found himself. He could not forget that he was bound by the word of the Lord, the very word which promised the safe return of God's dispersed people to Palestine, to settle and live and labour in Babylon as though he belonged there or would be there permanently, and to "seek the peace of the city whether the Lord had carried him away captive" (Jer.29:4-7). It was here that the righteousness of Mordecai and Daniel and many more like them shone most clearly. They could not be accused justly of anarchy or any form of seditious or subversive activity against the state under whose jurisdiction they were (cf.Dan.6:4). Rather, with Paul they were subject to the higher powers, knowing that there is no power but from God; the powers that be being ordained of God (Rom.13:1); and together with him they made "supplications, prayers, intercessions and thanksgivings for the king and all that are in authority; that they might live quiet and peaceable lives in all godliness and honesty, knowing that that was acceptable in the sight of God their Saviour" (I Tim.2:1-3). Obedience to all that was behind Mordecai's action of reporting the intentions of the would-be assassins of the king to him through Esther (Esth.2:21-23). His righteousness is seen to be genuine because, and only because, it was acted out before God as it was toward men, namely, according to the spirit as well as the letter of the commandment of the Lord. Conversely, as it is not possible to be righteous before God without due regard for one's fellows, neither can one act righteously toward one's neighbours without first taking one's obligations to God into consideration. So with Mordecai. When Ahasuerus promoted Haman to the chief place among his princes, he bestowed on him a kind of spurious divinity which all absolute monarchs and caesars arrogated to themselves. Men were expected to do obeisance before them, conduct which was tantamount to worship. This Mordecai refused to do before Haman (Esth.3:2). He was a Jew and such conduct was repugnant to him, being forbidden by the law of his God. The law was quite unequivocal when it stated in the words of the Lord Jesus, "Thou shalt worship the Lord thy God, and him only shalt thou serve" (Matt.4;10 cf. Ex.20:1-6). The love Mordecai had for his God was the basis of his love for his fellowmen; the service he rendered to his God embraced his service for his fellows; the worship he gave to his God determined that he treat men as men and not as God. Mordecai would not, could not bow a worshipping knee to Haman. That proud man might rage and fume and threaten, but God had spoken, "Them that honour me, I will honour; and they that despise me shall be lightly esteemed" (I Sam.2:30). In the light of that God had settled the issue before it had begun. Because of their respective attitudes toward God the positions of these two men would be reversed. The destruction Haman planned for Mordecai and his people fell upon himself (Esth.7:10); the promotion the king conferred upon Haman was transferred to Mordecai (Esth.10:2,3).

Haman was of royal descent, the princely remnant of what had once been a proud and powerful state, Amalek. How influential that kingdom had been in its day may be gathered from the words of Balaam when he prophesied of Jacob's future greatness, saying, "His king shall be higher than Agag, and his kingdom shall be exalted" (Num.24:7). The Amalakites were antagonistic to the Jews, possessed of an inveterate hatred of Israel. This was the nation which attacked Israel in a most cowardly fashion when she was on her way to the Promised Land. In the words of Moses, "Amalek met thee in the way, and smote the hindmost of thee, even all that were feeble behind thee, when thou wast faint and weary; and he feared not God" (Deut.25:17 cf. Ex.17:8). This was a crime God Himself never forgot, and would not permit His people to forget until it had been avenged. From the days of Moses down to the reign of Hezekiah this people was in constant conflict with Israel, often allying themselves with the Jews' enemies in their attempt to eradicate the chosen people from the face of the earth. They were twice defeated by Saul, but he incurred the divine anger by failing to eliminate them when commanded by God to do so (I Sam.15). Later, David inflicted a most humiliating defeat on them, a defeat which virtually destroyed their influence as a nation (I Sam.30), a destruction which was completed by Hezekiah, following which no further mention is made of them in Scripture. Haman was a direct descendant of the kingly line, Agag (Esth.3:1), and he inherited all his ancestors' hatred of the Jews. The description of him in Esther chapter 3, verse 10, "the Jews' enemy" was not what he became because of what Mordecai was doing or not doing to him, but what he had been always, and had never troubled to hide. It is not a reading into the text what is not there to say that those who informed on Mordecai to him did so maliciously because they knew of this hatred, and then sat back sadistically to await the outcome (Esth.3:3,4). They had not long to wait. Ignoring Mordecai contemptuously, Haman planned an empire wide campaign to have all the Jews exterminated on one day. By this campaign he did not hope nor did he expect to revive the former glories of Amalek, but to avenge the humiliation and the disgrace Israel had inflicted on his race (Esth.3:6; 9:24). But as far as Haman was concerned the writing was already on the wall. It is seen in what Zeresh, his wife and his advisers said to him when he told them of his degrading experience of organising and leading a procession in honour of Mordecai. They said, "If Mordecai be of the seed of the Jews, before whom thou hast begun to fall, thou shalt not prevail against him, but shall surely fall before him" (Esth.6:13). They, at any rate, had understood the message of history, namely, that God had spoken truly when He said of the seed of Abraham, "I will bless them that bless you, and curse him that curseth you" (Gen.12:3). As the servant of the Lord from Whom he had received his righteousness, Mordecai had this heritage, "No weapon that is formed against you shall prosper" (Isa.24:17). The sentence had already gone forth from the mouth of the Lord. From the very outset Haman and his cause were doomed to failure and destruction.

2. God and Haman.

The section of the Book of Esther under review contrasts God and Haman also. Of course, God is not mentioned by name, is not seen; but who with the scripture of truth in his hand can doubt either His presence or His influence? Both the Lord and Haman were planners; both had their own ends in view, both were meticulous in their preparations, but there the similarities end. Their respective plans bring them into opposition. If one succeeds the other will be destroyed. God knows how strong the opposition is and what its weaknesses. Haman is not aware there is an opposition, knows nothing of God, does not know he is fighting against God, is so blind in his own conceits he cannot conceive a stronger, more intelligent opponent planning to frustrate and defeat him. There is no evidence of such an enemy; at least, he sees none. But this invisible, secretly active God is always one step ahead of him, is actually using Haman's methods of planning to bring about his downfall. Haman, seated on the molehill of a king's favour, sees what he wants to see and cannot appreciate that it is a mirage or a castle of vapour built upon a foundation of chance.The kingdom of God has a secret service staffed by innumerable intelligence agents. So secret is it, that those citizens who benefit from its operations are least aware of it until much later, and its agents are so heavily disguised they seem to be nothing more than the ordinary, innocuous commonplace things of life. Did Mordecai think of this intelligence agency when a seemingly chance remark, a tip-off from a disgruntled servant, or the suspicious whisperings of Bigthan and Teresh suggested to him that evil was afoot, led him to uncover the traitors' foul intention and report the matter to the king through Esther? I daresay not, but without doubt Providence was at work, God's spies were active and regicide was averted. Ironically, it could be that, when the plot was uncovered, Haman was loudest in his condemnation of the villians and noisiest in his relief that the king's life had been spared, such was his fawning determination to gain favour; yet the exposure of the wicked intent was the precursor of his own downfall. The amazing wisdom of God! But the unknown, unseen agents were not finished with the matter. The hero of the hour, Mordecai was unsung, unrewarded. A very, very strange omission for those days, given the circumstances. The civil servants simply recorded the incident and, then, typically it was forgotten. Why? Perhaps the relief of the court was so great, or officials became engrossed with arranging a special sacrifice of thanksgiving to the local god, or maybe internal political struggles which necessitated a cabinet reshuffle (cf.Esth.3:1) were so urgent that all else was forgotten. At any rate, Mordecai received no commendation for his loyalty. Probably, he neither wanted or expected any; nonetheless, the oversight was most unusual. It was the Lord's doing. He chose to forget and it was forgotten; but when God remembers to forget, it is that He might not forget to remember to bless in His own time and way (Esth.2:21-23). God had made His next move.

Haman, eagerly seizing the opportunity the behaviour of Mordecai offered him to be rid of the Jews once and for all, set about planning the most suitable time for the massacre. He did not trouble to plan the destruction itself. That was the easy part. A bit of flattery, a few half-truths or untruths whispered in the ear of the monarch in whose eyes he could do no wrong, and backed by a substantial bribe to the king who was perpetually hard-up, and the standing army would do the rest (Esth.3:8-11). No need for Haman to dirty his hands; but according to the superstition of the day and place, the success of such an adventure depended on right timing. It was imperative that the right day, its exact date in the month, and the right month and year be known. The stars and the planets must be in a proper relation to each other if success were to be achieved, and these could be determined by pur, the casting of a small marked stone or dice. So confident was Haman of securing the king's consent that he actually set about determining the date before making any approach to the throne to get the requisite authority. Painstakingly the dice was cast, and the time chosen was eleven months ahead, the thirteenth day of the twelfth month (Esth.3:7,13). Such a far off date was no doubt necessary to allow time to alert the provinces and prepare the army, but, more importantly, it gave time for counter measures to be introduced. Had the massacre been planned for a few days ahead, the Jews could have offered no resistance, there being little time to change the king's mind. It was the right time, the time chosen by God. His was the unseen hand that controlled the roll of the dice. Man might cast the lot into the lap "but the disposing thereof is of the Lord" (Prov.16:33). God had made His final preparatory move. The scene was now set for the enacting of one of the most notable and glorious victories over the enemies of His covenant.

3. Ahasuerus' Inconsistent Conduct.

Ahasuerus consistently catered to his own security and comfort, but he was most inconsistent when dispensing justice. When Esther informed him that his life was threatened, he immediately took steps to have the matter investigated (Esth.2:23). We can be sure that no stone was left unturned until all the facts had been brought to light and the culprits executed. But when Haman accused the Jews of being rebellious and a constant threat to the king's safety and that of his realm and promised a large sum of money to expdite the eradication of the so-called rebels, Ahasuerus did not order an inquiry. With indecent haste he abrogated his authority to Haman, giving him permission to do with the Jews as he pleased (Esth.3:8-11); and Haman did not waste any time. The monarch did not require to exert himself. He was left to recline in comfort, as it were, knowing that for the time being he was financially solvent. And justice flew out of the window. But even this was under the control of the righteous Judge of all the earth. It would lead to the slaughter of a multitude of the Jews' enemies throughout the king's territories.

A great deal has been said, and is being said, of the harsh character of the righteousness, justice and wrath of God as portrayed in the Old Testament. It is claimed that this God is not the God of the New Testament; but those who make that claim must either read the New Testament with eyes and minds tightly shut or have erased from the Gospels particularly large portions of the teaching of Jesus and many of His sayings. His revelation of God is much more severe than that of the sternest of the prophets, and was so because He together with the prophets kept the truth concerning God in strict perspective. No lopsided view of the God of love and of the love of God came from His lips. His God was holiness and righteousness, truth and justice, grace and mercy at one and the same time, and every expression and exercise of His Godhead was a perfect balance of all these attributes. In no context from either the Old or the New Testament, where the person and activity of God are the theme, is there seen an excess of holiness to the detriment of love, an emphasis on mercy to the weakening of justice. Always He is presented as a just God and a Saviour (Isa.45:21). Being the Saviour of His people, having sealed His covenant concerning them with the precious blood of the only Son of His love, and by the shedding of this blood having satisfied the demands of His holiness, righteousness, wrath and love respecting them, He is just in all His dealings with those who are opposed to His redeemed and despise His grace. His redeemed are the apple of His eye (Zech.2:8), precious but very vulnerable; so He takes the utmost precautions to protect and preserve them, permits no man to do them wrong, reproves kings for their sakes, and has uttered this most solemn warning, "Touch not my anointed, and do my prophets no harm" (Ps.105;14,15). Where this warning is ignored, there there is an attempted violation of His covenant, a breaching of basic human standards, a denial of civil rights, and none of these can God tolerate. And He is not tied to any one method of displaying His justice and wrath. Only occasionally in Scripture were there visitations of His judgments which could be called 'acts of God', such as the Deluge, the destruction of Sodom and Gomorrah, the plagues which fell on Egypt and the entombment of the sons of Korah. As often as not, there seemed no direct involvement by God. Men suffered the same fate at the hands of their enemies which they had meted out to others. Adonibezek is a case in point. He had the unpleasant habit of cutting off the thumbs and great toes of the kings he conquered, and that is what the tribe of Judah did to him when they defeated and captured him. He said, "Three score and ten kings, having their thumbs and great toes cut off, gathered their meat under my table; as I have done so the Lord hath requited me" (Jud.1:7). Others fall foul of their own schemes. The Psalmist wrote of an enemy, "He made a pit and digged it, and is fallen into the ditch which he has made" (Ps.7:5); and as we have stated already, that is precisely what happened to Haman. He had had built a gallows on which he planned to execute Mordecai, but it was he whom the king hanged there (Esth.7:10). That brings us back to the inconsistency of Ahasuerus. He refused justice to the Jews, but his indifference to the rights and wrongs of the accusations made against them and his self-centredness gave Haman, their implacable enemy, free rein to travel along the road on which God would meet him and vindicate His justice. In other words, God used the unjustifiable conduct of the king because He, God, would destroy Haman and deliver His people (cf.Deut.2:30; Josh.11:20).

4. The King, Haman and the City of Shushan.

True to type, having satisfactorily concluded their agreement in a face saving way for the king (Esth.3:10,11), it was time to relax. Ahasuerus and Haman sat down to drink. They caroused, probably within the privacy of the king's chambers, congratulating each other on their diplomacy, the air growing thicker with liquor fumes, asinine compliments and lewd jests. They had no thought for the needless, cruel suffering they would inflict shortly on innocent men, women and children, were indifferent to the long term harm which would be done to the economical, political, social and aesthetic life of the empire by a sudden purging of some of its best business and academic brains, were blind to a possible breakdown of law and order which might follow in the wake of the unrestricted slaughter of the defenceless. There was every likelihood that the mob running unrestrained would loot and fire the premises of those murdered and then, having tasted blood, turn their attention to other unfortunate aliens. No doubt, this besotted pair thought it would be time enough to cross these bridges when they came to them; mean time, it was an hour for careless conviviality. But outside, the atmosphere was tense with apprehension. "The city of Shushan was perplexed" (Esth.3:15).

The councillors who had not been consulted could not make sense of the unexpected decree. There was neither reason nor excuse for it. Although the Jews might be a strange people, keeping themselves very much to themselves, ever giving the impression they were superior to all others, often acting with an arrogance which suggested that they were the captors and not the captives, always hinting of a day when they would march back to their homeland in triumph, a suggestion which seemed to savour of subversive plottings. Yet, if there were such plottings, they were kept so carefully hidden that not the slightest glimmer of them had been seen. Openly, they were imaginative and energetic in business, honest in their dealings, men who prospered quickly, who were ever ready to help, and who could be trusted. With their coming there had been introduced into society a new set of ethical and moral values which were cleaning it up and making the towns and cities better places to live in. All in all, it had been a good day for the empire when these Jews were settled perforce in the community. Why this sudden decision to destroy what was good?

The rank and file of the citizens shared this perplexity. The Jews they knew personally, particularly from business contacts, were in the main decent people. They might keep themselves separate, particularly at weekends which they called sabbaths, and at other times of the year in order to worship their unseen God and to celebrate their own peculiar religious festivals, but they were not stand-offish, not unapproachable. They took a keen interest in communal affairs which had no association with religion, were unashamed to speak of their God and His goodness, even while confessing that they were in exile because He was punishing them severely for their forgetfulness of Him and rebellion against His law. Whenever they spoke of their God, it was with obvious reverence, unlike the devotees of other religions, and always they made their God and religion attractive. So sincere was their faith and so exemplary their lives, many felt an urge to join them and not a few did. Those who resisted the urge, generally did so because of the strange initiatory rites which were imposed upon the converts together with the requirement that they forego many customs and activities familiar to them from childhood, in which they saw no harm, which were pleasing to the senses and made them the same as everyone else around them. Religion apart, the Jews were an essential part of the community and had given no cause to warrant their mass execution. It was madness.

Public opinion was against the decree, but it was not a day when public opinion was taken too seriously. The majority was reckoned to be the minority, and the minority, especially when that minority was an absolute monarch, was an overwhelming and irresistable majority. Yet, public opinion was not without its influence. We have seen already that the king, being very much a creature of the moment, acted on impulse, only to regret what he had done when the cost became apparent and it was too late to alter what he had decreed. So, on this occasion, another drunken orgy behind him, the disquiet of his courtiers, the silent sympathy of the business world toward the Jews, reports of which would infiltrate into the palace, were as a douche of cold water to him, sobering him, making him reflective, apprehensive, rueful. "If only....", but the decree of the Medes and Persians could not be changed. There was no open condemnation of the king, no hint of rebellion, just a sullen silence of disapproval which pressed heavily upon him, forcing him into a position in which he would gladly seize the slightest pretext to undo the wrong. All that may be gathered from the wrathful alacrity with which he responded to Esther's accusation of Haman (Esth.7:5-7), and the manner in which the Gentile community rallied to the support of the Jews when the counter decree permitted the Israelites to defend themselves (Esth.9:2,3). His own past experience and the covert opposition to his pact with Haman allied together to rudely awaken the monarch to the seriousness of the situation. Standing there in the queen's boudoir with the terror stricken Haman grovelling at his feet, the king thought, "What a fool I have been; made the willing tool of this scheming, contemptuous wretch before me. I have been in danger of losing another queen whom I love dearly, and have sown the seeds of disquiet within my court and in the country which could easily blossom into civil unrest, if not war". God's secret service had manouevred another great coup.

When the covenant of God is threatened, when the Church seems to be teetering on the verge of annihilation, when personal disaster looms large for the children of God and seems inescapable, then is the time to remember God's secret service. He is the God Who neither slumbers nor sleeps, Who is continually directing and using His agents to halt and defeat the forces of evil. Only so far are they allowed to go before He sweeps them back. The methods He uses may be very simple, of seemingly no significance in themselves, so commonplace and in no way related to the matter in hand, that none, not even those directly concerned, know that God will use such means to bring about the downfall of the evil and the triumph of the right. From out of such weakness comes the power which destroys the best laid schemes of devils and men. Of course, it must be in God's time. Often the waiting can be most harrowing, and demands will be made which are most traumatic - more of that later - but the Church's and the Christian's waiting time is God's working time, and He never keeps His people waiting one moment longer than is necessary. They must wait while His agents are at work, preparing for the deliverance, the blessing, the answer to prayer being sought. So God informed Daniel. In Daniel's day the state and plight of the people were very precarious and he was most anxious for their welfare. For three weeks he had wrestled before God on their behalf, and throughout those twenty-one days heaven was silent. His anxiety increased daily, sapping energy from his body and mind until he was almost a physical wreck. Then there came the word of the Lord through an angel: "O Daniel, a man greatly beloved, understand the words that I speak unto thee, and stand upright; for unto thee am I sent....Fear not, Daniel, for from the first day thou didst set thy heart to understand, and to chasten thyself before thy God, thy words were heard, and I am come for thy words. But the prince of the kingdom of Persia withstood me one and twenty days; but lo, Michael, one of the chief princes came to help me, and I remained there with the kings of Persia. Now I am come to make thee understand what shall befall thy people...." (Dan.10:11-14). Daniel's prayer offered in repentance and humility had been heard when first uttered, but before it could be answered, God had other work to do which would make the right answer possible. The Lord was operating elsewhere for His people's benefit.

This is the glory of Providence: it works in ways which are neither seen, known nor understood, and sometimes working in places afar off, that God might bring near at the right time the grace His people require.

ACCORDING TO PURPOSE

V

PRAYER AND PROVIDENCE

A young man in his thirties and a Christian of but a few years standing, being of an enquiring mind, found himself entangled with the perennial problem of God's predestination and man's free will. Unable to reconcile the two to his own satisfaction, he was convinced that it was an either/or situation, that he must accept one and reject the other. He decided in favour of God's predestination and later confessed, "I have stopped praying. If God knows all that will happen to me, if He has predestinated it, there is nothing I can do about it; so, why pray?" Apart from being a very narrow, lopsided view of prayer which confines it to "an asking for things" that knows nothing of communion with God, it is an embracing of the dangerous error of fatalism. It is dangerous because, rather than imparting a humble, contented submission to the will of God in the confidence that all things are being made to work together for good, it cultivates a stoicism, a hardness of heart which brings one into conflict with the workings of the Lord. Easy to sit back and happily take what is good. But when circumstances and conditions are adverse, to grit the teeth and say, "What must be will be", is to evince a spirit of indifference or bitterness which is the equivalent of taking to heart the advice of Job's wife to curse God and die. Mercifully, the young man has had his views corrected and is progressing satisfactorily along a more orthodox way.

Without entering into the freewill controversy or making any attempt to reconcile divine predestination and human responsibility, the Bible links prayer and Providence, and so too does the man of faith. he who prays, "Not my will but thine be done," and knows in his heart that God's will will be done, nonetheless, thanks God fervently when that will is performed in response to his prayers, sees a connection between the prayer and the answer. This inter-relationship of prayer and Providence is seen in the Book of Esther.

When the dreadful news broke that a day had been appointed on which all Jews would be exterminated, they resorted as one man to the throne of grace, where they could expect mercy and grace to help in their time of need (Heb.4:16). Their reaction to the king's brutal decree is recorded in chapter 4, verses 1 to 3. The rent clothes, the wearing of sackcloth and the sprinkling of ashes on the head or lying on beds of sackcloth and ashes, the fasting and the lamentable cries were not an ostentatious display of grief, though undoubtedly grief was present, a wearing of the heart on the sleeve to evoke the pity of men, but a graphic account of their approach to, and standing before, God during this time of crisis. It is not our way of coming before God in times of great stress. Fasting is sanctioned by the New Testament and many still practise it, but the Lord Jesus insisted that faith is of the heart, that our drawing near to God must be the heart approach, that the coming to God and any fasting which might accompany it must be in secret, and that the God Who is concerned only with the heart approach and Who sees its secret rewards openly (Matt.6:5,6,16-18). That is not to condemn the Jews for what some might consider extravagant piety. The Faith practised in the Old Testament, and as taught by the saints of that economy, is that taught in the New Testament and practised by Christians. It is the fruit of the covenant of grace, is founded on the person and work of the Lord Jesus Christ and experienced through faith in Him. But being before the time of the historical Christ, it was revealed to the Jews through external and material things such as the Tabernacle or Temple, its festivals, sacrifices and ritual. All these were types or figures foreshadowing the reality, Christ, and as such were aids to faith in Him, helping the instructed worshipper to look through and beyond them to the coming Messiah. So doing, they experienced the spiritual blessedness which He brought. The Faith being embodied in material things, personal faith was expressed in a physical way. The constant bringing of sacrifices for the remission of sins was token of their reconciliation to God and their need of continual cleansing (cf.I John 1:9). Their offering of the first fruits of the harvest field, of the farm and the family and the tithing of their incomes were the evidence that they and theirs were wholly the Lord's and holy to Him. Similarly, their approach to God in times of great stress was marked by physical characteristics such as are described in Esther chapter 4 and elsewhere. That does not mean that all who engaged in these exercises were men of faith. In every generation there were those for whom the practice of fasting was nothing more than a barren duty; others were like the Pharisees who made a pretence of it in order to be seen of men. But when fasting and its accompaniments were from the heart of faith, they were acceptable to God. They depicted the true state of the souls before Him; revealed the broken and contrite spirit which He never despises.

Fasting played an important role in the religious life of the Jews. There were stated fasts associated with the observance of the Day of Atonement (Lev.16:29,31 etc) or held at set times throughout the year (cf.Zech.8:19). Perhaps these would tend to be of a formal character, but when we recall that Moses, when receiving the law from God on Mount Sinai, fasted forty days and forty nights (Ex.34:28; Deut.9:9), it can be appreciated that fasting, even formal fasting, was ordained to prevent the things and concerns of earth and time coming between the suppliant and his communion with his God. However, fasting was seen at its most significant when the people were confronted with some national, religious or personal crisis. It was the way by which they approached to cast themselves on His mercy. At such times fasting, as may be gathered from its accompanying lamentations and the wearing of, or lying on, sackcloth and ashes, was not merely abstention from food and drink, but from the domestic, business and social activities of the day. It was quite literally an afflicting of the soul (Lev.16:29,31; 23:27,32; Ezra 8:21 etc.). But why fasting? It was a sign of the people's sincerity. They were intimating in the most practical way they knew that they meant business coming before God in the manner they did.

It meant also, as it did on more formal occasions, that they were permitting no earthly, temporal or physical distractions interfering with their supplications. So urgent was their need, it was inconceivable that they should think in terms of what was otherwise normal and important; so vital was God's response to them that they were willing to surrender all natural desires in order to seek it. Fasting, they were acknowledging that they esteemd the will and blessing of God more than their necessary food.

Fasting implied helplessness in the face of a particular situation, a being at wits end corner (cf.Ps.107:27), a not knowing which way to turn, a placing of oneself before God for Him to do as He pleased, knowing that He is the God of mercy Who "will repent himself concerning his servants" (Ps.135:14). David, helpless before the illness which was draining away the life of his first-born by Bathsheba, gave himself to fasting as he supplicated for the life of his child (II Sam.12:16-23); Jehoshophat confronted with the overwhelming war machine of Moab and Ammon proclaimed a national fast (II Chron.20:1-4), for he knew that at that time the people had no help but in God; Ezra confident that the Lord could lead His people back from exile without the protection of a pagan king's escort, called them to fast in order to demonstrate their total dependence on the Lord (Ezra 8:21-23).

Generally speaking, lamentations, loud cryings and the wearing of, and the lying on, sackcloth and ashes accompanied the fasting. This conduct symbolised humbling themselves before God, the adopting the position of penitents as they made confession of sin, a necessary preamble as they waited upon God for the required mercy (Dan.9:3-5). In brief, fasting was an act of repentance. Repentance is a confession of sins which denotes true godly sorrow for what is admitted, a holy determination to break away from what is confessed and to be more faithful to God and to righteousness in the future. It is a dying more unto known sin and a living more in obedience to the revealed will of God. But that does not complete the make-up of this grace. It contains another ingredient which is often overlooked, namely, it is a waiting upon God to do with us as He pleases, knowing that, however He responds, it will be wisely and lovingly, and that humbly His dealings with us must be accepted. For example, David fasted before God pleading for the life of his son, but God chose that the infant should die. When the child expired, David to the amazement of his servants immediately forsook the trappings of grief and returned to a normal life. He explained, "While the child was yet alive, I fasted and wept; for I said, Who can tell whether the Lord will be gracious to me, that my child should live? But now he is dead, wherefore should I fast? Can I bring him back again? I shall go to him, but he shall not return to me" (II Sam.12:22,23). That is true repentance, the spirit of the penitent Job who said from the midst of the ashes, "What? shall I receive good at the hand of the Lord and not evil? Yea, though he slay me, yet will I trust in him" (Job 2:10; 13:15). That is the voice which is heard when the heart fasts before the Lord.

The fasting of the Jews in Esther's day was occasioned by what seemed adverse

Providences, but it was not as bad as the people feared. We know that God had already set in motion a chain of circumstances which would give them a happy issue out of their present distress, but they did not know that. This history sets the conduct of the people against the background of God's secret workings, that generations to come might be able to view similar situations in which they find themselves from two angles, from God's viewpoint and the Church's. On the one hand there is the anxious praying of the people, and on the other the Providence of God which is never still on behalf of His suppliants. One of the most important lessons to be learned here is that those coming to God with the urgent need and desire to cast all their care upon Him have the assurance that even before they had need to pray God had set about answering them, that even while they are calling upon Him He is responding to their cry. Another truth suggested here is that as it is by means of Providences the Lord's children are led into their dark valleys, so in the same way are they led out of darkness and into the light. This answering of prayer by providential means is one which the majority of Christians accept and expect. In the Scriptures God seldom intervenes in the affairs of His people by direct miraculous methods which take no account of, or set aside the course of, nature and the actions of men. The dividing of the waters of the Red Sea, so that they stood up like walls of glass to permit the Jews to walk dry-shod to the other side, and the neutralising of the super heated furnace into which Daniel's three companions were flung are two of the many examples of God's immediate, miraculous deliverance of His people, but in the main He uses the forces of nature and the activities of men, the latter usually unwittingly on their part. Christians should expect this; nonetheless, when plunged suddenly into the crises which threaten their well being and that of the Church, the Lord expects them to react as did the Jews, and they invariably do. They have resort to prayer, pray earnestly and passionately, as did the Israelites, and learn all over again that prayer and Providence are inextricably bound together, that Providence prompts prayer, that prayer itself is providential, and that the blessings of Providence come through prayer.

The Jews prayed as they did because they were perplexed. They could not understand the sudden and unexpected turn of events. They went to bed as contented, comfortable, prosperous and secure as any exiles could be; in fact, as those who were regarded almost as natives by their neighbours; and they awoke to the threat of extermination. Why? They had offended no state law or institution or regulation. Was God angry with them and about to punish them as never before? And if so, why? Their perplexity drove them to God and repentance; to repentance, because their bewilderment would lead to soul searching in the presence of the holiness of God. Who can stand in that light and not be aware of sin within? Those Jews were no exception. They did not stand and say, ''God, we thank you that we are not as other men; we do not deserve your frown, not as these pagan Persians among whom we are forced to live.'' No! They were on their faces before Him, suddenly aware that they were not as they should be, that if the Lord should mark iniquity, they could not stand before Him. Riches had increased and they were setting their hearts on them. Prosperity had made them complacent and the worship of God was losing much of its significance and blessing. Their acceptance as good neighbours by the Persians had dulled somewhat their remembrance of their homeland, had blurred their vision of the hope of the covenant. The bitter truth was stabbing at their hearts, making them painfully aware that they were not as single minded as they might be in seeking first the kingdom of God and His righteousness, that in many unobtrusive ways, which they themselves had failed to recognise, they had not attended to the good required of them, had been more concerned with the evil they should have left untouched. In that awe-full Presence the nagging thought, "Why should this happen to us?" gave way to the humiliating, "Why has it not happened before?" How wretched they were. Their mournful cry was, "God be merciful to us, sinners." There is a close connection between Providence and soul health. Adverse circumstances which strike suddenly should promote a healthy self examination. They are the Good Physician's methods of diagnosing for His people the soul sicknesses of which they may be unaware. They consider themselves healthy, but deep inside viruses are at work which, if not dealt with, can lead to painful and excessive soul damage, if not death. The adversities which drive to God in perplexity are good providences when they lead to repentance and a closer walk with God. The Psalmist acknowledged, "It was good for me that I was afflicted; for thou in thy faithfulness hath afflicted me with all thy waves that I might keep thy statutes; and this is my comfort in affliction, thy word hath quickened me, and now I keep thy word" (Pss.88:7; 119:50,67,71,75,107).

It was stated earlier that repentance includes willingness to submit to the will of God, but what that will was was hidden from the Jews when violence first threatened. Their fasting, then, was a confession of ignorance. Brought to lie before God with broken and contrite hearts, they could not see, did not know how God would work; and even when Mordecai persuaded Esther to intercede with the king, very few were cognisant of it. They were completely in the dark. They could only pray and wait. This ignorance is most difficult to bear. Faced with the seemingly impossible, painfully aware of impotence, yet the mind racing on, considering this or that course of action, and rejecting each in turn as futile. Every muscle and limb straining to do something when there is nothing that can be done, and all the while not knowing if anything is being attempted elsewhere. All this can have a most debilitating effect upon the soul. Spiritual energy drains away, hope grows dim and there is near despair. That is the worst feature of the type of prayer we are considering, yet prayer continues to be offered. The classic example of this is the church in Jerusalem praying earnestly and constantly for Peter awaiting execution in Herod's prison, but without any expectation of his release (Acts 12:1-16). This is one of the most amazing paradoxes of prayer: the more hopeless it seems the more fervently it is engaged in. The reason for this is not far to seek. It is found in "the witness within" which the believer has (I John 5:10). He who confesses his sins, being truly repentant, has a strong inner sense of peace, of condemnation having been removed, of oneness with God. The Holy Spirit is bearing witness with his spirit assuring him that he is a child of God (Rom.8:16). This in turn leads to the conviction that though he does not know what to pray for as he ought, and that his attempts at prayer sound like incoherent groanings and gropings after God and the knowledge of His will, yet the supplication is not in vain. He Who has the mind of God, the Holy Spirit, is making direct contact with the throne of grace through the groanings, making the incoherent coherent, placing the stumbling, imperfect petitions in the hands of the Church's great High Priest, Who makes them perfect in His perfect, ceaseless intercessions for His people. That makes for peace; for "this is the confidence we have in him, that if we ask anything according to his will, he heareth us" (I John 5:14).

Confidence is the companion of perplexity and ignorance when the children of God pray in a time of sudden crisis. It is the assurance that because they are the Lord's, He will never leave them nor forsake them, that He will be their helper, that He has no change of heart respecting them, that He continues to purpose their good. And it is a confidence centred in His Providence. They know that "the earth is the Lord's and the fulness thereof; the world and all that dwell therein" (Ps.24:1). For the Church that is not simply an affirmation of the credal statement that God is the Maker of heaven and earth, or an agreeing with the New Testament when it says that "by him all things were created which are in heaven and on earth, visible and invisible, whether they be thrones or dominions or principalities or powers; all things were created by him and for him" (Col.1:16). It goes further than that but not beyond the bounds of Scripture. It means that all creation is the Lord's to use or dispense with as He pleases. It is a confidence which sees nothing capricious in the movements of nature and which dismisses as puerile the boastful claims of man that he is sovereign, "the monarch of all he surveys, the master of his fate, and the captain of his soul." It is a confidence founded on the doings of the Lord. The incarnate Son of God, the Creator saw a fig tree which promised to satisfy His hunger, but it offered not figs but leaves. He there and then condemned it, and it withered and died (Matt.21:18,19). How the critics have raved about that. "If Christ did do that, and it is doubtful, what right had He?" He did do it; and His was the right of ownership, the right to get rid of what was His because He knew it to be useless. The destruction of the herd of swine at Gadara may be viewed in a similar light (Matt.9:28-34), but, if possible, that incident has angered the critics even more. The fig tree probably was wild and nobody's property, but those swine belonged to men, were their wealth and livelihood. Was Christ's the action of a caring, loving God? Do these people not know that it is written, "Every beast of the forest is mine, and the cattle on a thousand hills"? (Ps.20:10 cf. Hag.2:8). Whatever lessons these incidents were intended to teach, and they are many - the most notable among them being that prayer is a most powerful weapon in the hands of him who believes, and that in the sight of God one human soul is of infinitely greater value than a herd of swine (cf.Matt.12:12) - this they do impress upon us: nature and whatever man has is at the disposal of the Lord, and that always there is good in His disposing. The same truth is evident from God's dominion over nations and men. Nowhere is this more clearly seen than in His donating the Promised Land to the children of Israel. When the promise was first given to Abraham, and at the time of the Exodus from Egypt, Canaan was inhabited by peoples who considered it their own; but they were overcome and destroyed, not so much by the military might of Israel as by the hand of God, to make room for the Twelve Tribes. Moses reminded the people that they would not acquire the land by their own strength, that it was an inheritance from the Lord, given originally to their fathers because He loved them; and that in keeping with that promise He would drive out the original inhabitants who were numerically, physically and militarily superior (Gen.12:7; Deut.4:38; Amos 2:9). The Jews were never permitted to forget that Canaan was the Lord's provision (Ex.6:8; Josh.1:2), and that it was He Who led them forty years through the wilderness to it (Amos 2:10). It must be added, however, that the land never ceased to be the Lord's, that it was given to Israel in trust, and that they were under constant threat of expulsion should they fail that trust (Lev.18:28; Deut.4:26,38; 30:17,18). Every reader of the Old Testament knows how abysmally Israel failed. She did not totally expunge the land of its former inhabitants and their corrupt practices. These and the influence of surrounding nations polluted the moral and religious life of the Jews to such an extent they could scarcely be distinguished from the heathen, and the fate which came upon the Cananites fell upon the Hebrews. They were expelled from the land because they had not kept faith with God. The first expulsion was for a short period only, seventy years, until the land had recovered from its maltreatment at Jewish hands (cf. II Chron.36:21) and the people purged of idolatory. But the second banishment was more prolonged, followed shortly after their rejection and crucifixion of Jesus Christ, was a scattering of the majority across the face of the earth, and may well prove permanent. True, the Jews still retain their racial identity, still look for their Messiah, still have great national aspirations, and in part have returned and taken possesion of a portion of the land that was once theirs. But there are more Jews outside of Palestine than in it, and religiously and politically they are so far removed from what God ordained, it is debateable whether they will ever take complete possession of the inheritance. Strictly speaking, even if repossession were achieved, it would be of little significance. While the earth and its fulness still remain the Lord's, His holy nation is no longer a peopled land but the Church of Christ (cf.I Pet.2:9), and Israel's expectation of knowing the blessings of the promises lies in her citizens being incorporated into the Church through faith in and submission to the Lord Jesus Christ (see Rom.11:23-27). To that must be added that the Church is under constant obligation to preach the gospel to the Jew first (Rom.1:16). But to return to the eviction and destruction of the Canaanite tribes: God did not act arbitrarily when dealing with these peoples as He did. He executed His justice upon them. For centuries they had lived as those described by Paul in Romans chapter 1, verse 18 to 32. Wilfully and culpably they rejected God and the basic standards of humanity and righteousness, had invented idolatrous schemes of religion which debased human dignity and perverted man's finer instincts, particularly in the realms of human relationships. When God gave His covenant promise to Abraham, this depravity was well known, but He took no action. He informed Abraham that "the iniquity of the Amorites was not yet full" (Gen.15:16). Not yet had the wickedness of these peoples reached the point of no return. There was still time and opportunity for them to turn from their evil ways and unrighteous thoughts and to seek the Lord. Had they done so He would have pardoned them abundantly. Here is an instance of the longsuffering grace of God. He was not willing these peoples should perish, gave them innumerable evidences of His wisdom and power, and waited to receive them. He waited until they themselves had made a return to Him impossible, and then, the very land they boasted was theirs and were determined to defend ejected them as unpalatable and dangerous (Lev.18:28).

"Ye shall keep my statutes and my judgments that the land vomit not thee out also, as it vomited out the nations which were before you". So said the Lord to Israel on the eve of their entrance into the Promised Land. A puzzling statement? The land was a good one, having a pleasant and secure situation, was rich and fertile and productive of all that was necessary to prosperous living. The Canaanite tribes had made the most if it, as was borne out by their size and strength, while the fortresses they built showed their determination to keep it (Num.13:28,33). Yet the land rejected them. How? It is obvious from the above statement from Leviticus, seen in context, that there is the closest possible correspondence between righteousness of life and national life, that they are so inter-related each acts upon and influences the other. Where the moral and ethical are given priority, there they blend and co-operate with the physical and temporal to produce a healthy, virile race, strong in character. Where the standards of righteousness are ignored, scorned and abused, there, however well fed and catered for the bodies, the race begins to lose character and sense of purpose. When bread and possessions and pleasures become the be-all and end-all of life, a silent, secret leaking of iron from the soul takes place, creating what Paul terms effeminacy or soft living, reducing the vitality of the nation and robbing it of the will and desire and the ability to cope with crises as they arise. How easily the Israelites ousted the Canaanites. The latter had no stomach for the fight. The conquest of Jericho vividly illustrates that. The Israelites simply tramped round the walls of the city once on each of six consecutive days and seven times on the seventh day and then saw the walls of the city collapse. The co-operation of nature? Not once during that week was a Jerichoan seen or heard, no spear or arrow was fired from the walls, no defensive measures were taken. The will to survive had perished. The land ejected its inhabitants. Another name for it would be the Providence of God. If the wages of sin is death, then the Lord had simply to leave the city to its own devices and nature did the rest. "Righteousness does exalt a nation, but sin is a reproach to any people" (Prov.14:34).

This over-ruling Providence of God working out His purpose for the good of His people is seen also in what might be termed the coincidences of life. Joshua sent two spies into Jericho. Their intelligence was vital to the success of his campaign (Josh.2:23,24), and it was a strange turn of events which protected them. They lodged in a brothel, there to learn that their identity was known to the security forces, and that the woman of the house impressed by what she had heard of Israel's exploits under their God, had become a believer in Jehovah and desired asylum with His people. So, having received a guarantee of safety from them, she hid the spies, gave them an escape route, and so they accomplished their mission successfully (Josh.2:1-24). Notice, too, the timing of Ruth's arrival in Bethlehem. Elimelech, his wife and two sons emigrated to Moab when famine hit Canaan. The sons married Moabitish women, then tragedy. Elimelech and his sons died leaving three widows. The famine having ended, Naomi, his widow decided to return home, and Ruth, widow of one of the sons, having been converted to the Jewish Faith, insisted on returning with her. They reached Bethlehem at the beginning of barley harvest (Ruth 1:22). The timing was significant. Naomi and Ruth, being poor, Ruth found it necessary to glean in the harvest fields in order to sustain Naomi and herself. The field she chanced to enter into belonged to Boaz, a wealthy farmer and a close relative of Elimelech's. Learning who she was, he provided amply for her and her mother-in-law, and came to love her. However, he could not take her to wife because Jewish law required that the nearest male relative should have that privilege so that Elimelech's line might be continued (Deut.25:5). This the nearer relative declined and Boaz was free to marry Ruth, which he did. Their firstborn proved to be the grandfather of David, thus instituting the Davidic line from which Messiah should come (Ruth 4:22). Coincidences are the tools of Providence.

So, too, is what the world calls chance. Samaria was under seige from Syria and famine was rife in the capital. Four lepers, denied entrance to the city, decided to visit the Syrian camp, knowing that if the Syrians refused to satisfy their hunger, they would be no worse off. When they reached the camp it was empty. Benhadad, the Syrian king, having received a report of rebellion in his own land, ordered his troops to return home in great haste, which they did, leaving behind all their supplies. The lepers feasted themselves full, then informed their fellow citizens, and the hunger of the city was assuaged. Luck? A few hours before the lepers visited the camp, Elisha had prophesied that the next day food would be in plentiful supply. Not luck, the Providence of God (II Kgs.7:1-16). Again, Micaiah prophesied that the king of Israel would be slain in battle and was imprisoned for his pains. But taking no chances, the king disguised himself that he might not be recognised by the enemy. However, we read, "A man drew a bow at a venture and smote the king of Israel between the joints of his armour" (I Kgs.22:34). The archer aimed at nothing but the arrow struck a vital target. Fluke? Yes, as far as the man was concerned, but an unseen hand directed the flight of the shaft. In both these instances prophecy indicated the purpose of God, and events were engineered to accomplish it.

With God nothing is impossible as He works to make good His covenant. He is the master craftsman who has to hand all the tools He requires, uses each as need arises and with perfect skill, and always finishes to His own satisfaction the task to which He commits Himself. Knowing that, His people can cast upon His care the most hopeless situations of life. It might be, of course, that He chooses to leave their cicumstance or condition unchanged, as He did when His answer to Paul's prayer for the removal of the latter's thorn in the flesh was no. That malady, whatever it was, remained with Paul to the end of his days, but not only did he learn to live with it, he discovered it was not the handicap he feared it might be, that what he thought was a curse proved to be a blessing. He received sufficient grace to overcome it, discovered God's strength in his weakness, and learned that his ailment was a means of glorifying Christ (II Cor. 12:5-10). The Scripture evidence we have given, and it could be extended considerably, teaches that the unlikely is likely because God can make all sorts of event, circumstances and conditions, however far off and unrelated to the needs which prompted the prayers of His people, so to synchronise that their requests are granted. In 1940 Britain prayed when her armies were trapped and seemed doomed in France. An evacuation was undertaken from Dunkirk, a mammoth task at the best of times but scarcely possible under assault conditions. But the sea, unusually calm for that time of the year, assisted a safe and triumphant withdrawal. In a way, that withdrawal marked a turning point of the war in the Allies' favour. Winston Churchill called it a miracle. It was the Providence of God at work through prayer. Crises bring the Church and her members boldly to the throne of grace knowing that grace and mercy can be expected from the Monarch of the universe. Having prayed, the suppliants must wait and watch for, and be prepared to respond to, the movements of Providence, knowing that God will bring all necessary resources into action to give an answer of peace.

ACCORDING TO PURPOSE

VI

INTELLIGENT PRAYER

Prayer and Providence go hand in hand. But how should we pray? Intelligently! Intelligent prayer is effective prayer. That might seem to run contrary to what was said in the previous chapter concerning the Christian's ignorance when praying during a time of apparent hopelessness. How can one pray intelligently when not sure how to pray? At such times effective prayer is dependent not so much on the words used or how the thoughts are expressed as on a right understanding of what it means to pray. There might be a confusion of thoughts and a groping for words, yet the person who is praying knows what he is about. Samuel Rutherford said that "words are the accidents of prayer", and that might be said of the thoughts also. What then is intelligent prayer? Definitions of prayer and praying are innumerable. Almost every practioner of the art of prayer has his own, and seen in the context in which he uses it, is more or less correct. We are concerned with supplication and intercession in a time of dire straits. There comes to mind two descriptions of prayer, the sources of which have slipped the memory, which apply to these departments of prayer, and may be drawn from Esther chapter 4, verse 4 through to chapter 5, verse 8. They are: "Until we have prayed there is nothing we can do, when we have prayed there is everything to be done"; and "Prayer is putting oneself in the hands of God and taking the consequences".

The section of the book now occupying our attention illustrates the effectiveness of intelligent supplication as practised by both Mordecai and Esther. They were supplications which obtained results, for one of the messages of the Book of Esther is that God does answer prayer. But before discussing our two quotations as summarising what is taught in this portion of the book, we must focus our attention on what is the first requisite of intelligent prayer, namely, faith; the faith that God is, and that He is the rewarder of them that diligently seek Him (Heb.11:6). The Lord Jesus Christ, Who Himself was a man of prayer, spoke of the prayer of faith as the most potent force available to His disciples (see Matt.7:7; 18:19; 21:22; Mk.11:24; Lk.11:9; John 14:13f; 15:7; 16:24). Prayer, He taught, must be offered in His name, voiced according to His will, and when breathed in faith is always heard and answered. Consequently, whatever else His followers can or cannot do, and particularly when there is nothing they can do, they must never cease to pray, and to pray persistently. They must pray as those who reverently demand an answer from God as their right, and who keep on praying until they get it (Lk.18:1). That was Mordecai at prayer. Though the king's decree was irreversible, though the problem was beyond human wit to solve, he prayed believingly, was convinced beyond all shadow of doubt that God would deliver His people. When urging Esther to intercede with the king, his reasoning was, "If this calamity overtakes us, you, even though you are the queen, will not escape. If you refuse to help, deliverance will come from another quarter, but you and yours will be destroyed" (Esth.4:13,14). Deliverance will come from another quarter. Mordecai's was a faith in the promises of God akin to that of Abraham's. That old patriarch was convinced that though at the command of God he sacrifice Isaac, the sole promised seed, God would honour His covenant by raising Isaac from the dead (Heb.11:17-19). Simple, earnest faith is essential to effective prayer. But intelligent faith recognises that the content of such prayer must be according to the will of God (I John 5:14). The prayer Jesus had in mind, the prayers of Abraham and Mordecai, were for the preservation of the covenant of grace, were that all the promises which are yea and amen in Christ Jesus might be fulfilled and experienced by His covenant people to the glory of God. That is the content and purpose of all true prayer whatever form it might take, whatever requests it might contain. Covenant blessing is all that matters, and any request that has not that end in view, if granted, is more of a judgment than a mercy, for it leads to leanness of soul (cf.Ps.106:15).

That brings us to the first of the quotations mentioned above. Let me remind you of it again. "Until we have prayed there is nothing we can do; when we have prayed, there is everything to be done." That was the philosophy of both Mordecai and Esther, and it is a sound one. As soon as Mordecai heard the grim news of the decreed destruction of his people, he had resort to prayer, not simply because there was nothing else he could do, but, understanding the seriousness, if not the hopelessness, of the situation, he knew his first and only help was God. Therefore, he must seek God first. But more importantly, perhaps, Mordecai knew that the mischief which had been planned was principally an attack on God's covenant. That made it God's concern. His glory was at stake. It was important, therefore, that the matter be referred to Him at the earliest possible moment for the attention of His wisdom, power and grace. Under the circumstances it would have been the height of impertinence to ignore Him, call upon Him as an afterthought or as a last resort. Hezekiah acted as did Mordecai, when he received the arrogant, blasphemous letter from Rabshakeh, Sennacherib's general, demanding the unconditional surrender of Judah to Assyria. "He went upto the house of the Lord, and spread the letter before the Lord" (II Kgs.19:14). This is one of the marks of the man of faith: prayer is his first priority. So important to Mordecai was this principle of taking the matter before the Lord first that he resisted all well meant efforts to take him from the throne of grace. Ignorant of the king's decree and distressed by the news of Mordecai's mourning, Esther had fresh clothing sent to him (Esth.4:4). She was inviting him to break his fast and to cease his lamentations. It was tantamount to saying, "The situation, whatever it is, cannot be as bad as you are making out, compose yourself and you will find the dilemma resolving itself in a day or two". Such counsel, and how plentiful it is, is like rubbing salt into a raw wound, so unthinking is it in its lack of understanding and sympathy. Before offering any advice to a distressed supplicant before God, care should be taken to understand something of the problem, and if understanding and experience cannot offer practical help, better to stand alongside the distressed soul in silent sympathy and in intercession for him at the throne of mercy. Mordecai rightly refused the unspiritual suggestion.

Enlightened as to the cause of Mordecai's grief, and finding herself inextricably involved in the crisis, Esther's first response was as her uncle's, prayer; but she went further. She requested that all the Jews in the capital join in supplication with her, while she held prayer meetings with her personal staff. Many of her retinue would not be Jews, but that they were attached to her person would make their loyalty to the state suspect should the purge take place, and they would perish with her. She invited all who were likely targets of Haman's devilry to share vigil with her before God. They formed an ideal prayer meeting. Their common danger, fears and desires bound them together in supplication, gave intensity to their requests, and held the promise of a just and gracious response from God. This is the promise: "If two of you shall agree on earth as touching anything you shall ask, it shall be done for you of my Father who is in heaven" (Matt.18:19). Daniel too knew the value of the joint intercessions of those who are the intended victims of any treacherous scheme. Nebuchadnezzar's absurd decision to execute all his councillors because they could not tell him what his forgotten dream was, involved Daniel and his three friends, Shadrach, Meshach and Abednego. When Daniel heard of the decree, he immediately called on his three companions "that they should desire mercies from the God of heaven concerning this secret; that Daniel and his fellows should not perish with the rest of the wise men of Babylon" (Dan.2:18). This little prayer meeting knew the blessing of answered supplications.

However, the statement "until we have prayed there is nothing we can do" is not strictly true, does not necessarily apply to every critical situation. Sometimes there is something we must do before we pray, or do it as we pray. For instance, Daniel knew nothing of the king's order to kill all the wise men of Babylon until the guard came to execute it on him. Diplomatically he suggested to the captain of the guard that perhaps the king was unthinkingly rushing matters and suggested a stay of execution until he had consulted with the king. This was agreed, the king's problem was solved and the foolish order cancelled (Dan.2:14-16). On that occasion action had to precede prayer, but knowing Daniel it is safe to assume that on the way to the palace and while consulting with the monarch, he was praying silently that the monarch would grant a temporary stay of execution. As with all else, so with prayer: circumstances must dictate the appropriate course of action, but all must be done in the spirit of prayer. That is intelligent prayer.

Having been driven before God by the threat of a catastrophe which, humanly speaking, could not be averted, what does one do next? Providence provides the answer. Mordecai seized on the opportunity Esther's approach to him gave of challenging her to go to her husband and have him rescind the murderous decree against the Jews. As he viewed it, this was Providence supporting Providence. It was not fortuitous that Esther had been appointed queen, nor was she enthroned for her own and her spouse's benefit alone. She was there because the good hand of God was upon her, and was it not possible that He had placed her in her present position in order to deal effectively with the crisis which had engulfed her people? Mordecai did not know, but he was sure that the appointment was more than coincidence. Naturally timid, inexperienced in political affairs, and aware of her husband's uncertain temper, Esther gave many valid reasons why it was both dangerous and useless for her to comply with Mordecai's suggestion. But she was too much of a Jewess to deny or shrug off the force of her uncle's arguments, and reluctantly consented to see the king with an almost fatalistic resignation, saying, "If I perish, I perish." First she prayed, knowing that that was her first priority, and prayed knowing that when she rose from her knees a great deal would be demanded of her, that the fate of her people was in her hands. It was then she learned the truth of the second of the two statements on prayer we have in mind, namely, that "prayer is putting oneself in the hands of God and taking the consequences."

It is a true assessment of prayer. In the Garden of Gethsemane the Lord Jesus with His "Not my will but thine be done" put Himself in the hands of God and the consequence was Calvary. Daniel, knowing that his political colleagues were thirsting for his blood, committed himself to God in prayer and then was forced to spend the night among hungry lions. Esther fasted fully aware that though she would go into the king's presence in the strength of the Lord, she could be going to certain death. Each of them prayed as those who had faced up to the facts as they saw them. They did not pretend that the danger and the dread did not exist; they did not ignore that what followed their praying would test their physical, mental and spiritual resources to the utmost; Esther and Daniel did not shut their eyes to their own limitations and frailties and the human tendency to shrink from pain, suffering and disgrace. Their praying took account of all these factors. That is to pray intelligently. They prayed also for the courage to go forward resolutely, sharing the confidence and determination shown by Shadrach, Meshach and Abednego when they faced the prospect of the fiercely heated furnace, "If it be so, our God whom we serve is able to deliver us; but if not" we will neither forsake, disown nor deny our faith (Dan.3:17,18). How edifying and stimulating such a rising from prayer is may be appreciated when contrasting it with the irrational conduct of Peter. Totally disregarding that he had proved himself to be weak and presumptuous, deafened by his own conceit to the counsel and warning of Christ, and blind to what was revealed of himself in the mirror of Him Who is the truth, Peter loudly boasted, "Though all men shall be offended because of thee, Lord, I will never be offended" (Matt.16:33). Made confident by his pharisaic prayer, he went forth boldly not to stand before a furnace heated to its maximun capacity but before a brazier of burning coals to keep himself warm, and to confront not the wrath of a despot but the mischievious tongue of a servant lass. The heat of the fire and the sting of the tongue were too much for him: the one melted his resolve, the other killed his courage and deflated his ego. In the most humiliating manner he denied his Lord. A reasoned supplication takes cognisance of all relevant circumstances and personal factors and weighs all against the grace and faithfulness of God, and concludes that God can neither fail nor hurt His loved ones unnecessarily. Where there is such praying, whatever the physical and temporal outcome of what occasioned the supplication, there, there is peace and faith is exonerated.

But we are concerned chiefly with Esther. Strengthened by prayer to meet whatever might be the outcome of her proposed action, she prepared to enter the presence of the king. If there was a fatalistic element in her reply to Mordecai, it had disappeared by the time she entered the throne room without a royal summons and unannounced. She had left nothing to chance or fate. She acted as intelligently following her prayer as she did while praying. If the lives of her fellow countrymen depended upon her, then she would bring into play all the weaponry of her womanly wiles to force a change of heart in the king. Prior to coming before her husband, she spent a long time on her toilette, using the finest cosmetics and perfumes to enhance every feature of her personal beauty. She then dressed herself in the grandest and the most becoming of creations the royal couturier's art could devise, and as a final touch she placed the royal crown upon her head. When she appeared suddenly in the audience chamber, elegant, regal, lovely and smiling shyly, the king saw her as he had never seen her before. He saw her outstanding feminine beauty in a new light, felt the sweet charisma of her presence, knew her to be his queen, his wife, was instantly aware how fortunate he was, was conscience stricken as he remembered how he had been neglecting her of late, as delight, desire and love welled up within him - and he held out the golden sceptre, symbol of his favour, toward her. Intelligent prayer leads to intelligent action which always gets results. One cannot imagine David going to fight Goliath without first committing himself to God, seeking both strength and direction from Him. Having done so, his next step was to concentrate on the tactics he would adopt. Saul, too scared to fight the giant himself, would encourage the stripling by generously lending him his armour, but David would have none of it. He went out not as a knight in shining armour two sizes too large for him, and falling over his own feet every step he took, but as what he was and knowing what he would do. He went out as he had done on other occasions when danger threatened, as a shepherd lad determined to defend his flock from a ruthless enemy. He was determined to fight to the best of his ability, using the weapons he knew best how to handle. Is it too much to say that God chose him to be king of Israel, knowing him to be a man after His own heart, one who would lead, provide for and defend the Lord's people as he had his herd of sheep, wisely, courageously, selflessly? He behaved naturally and intelligently, as did Esther, and both won the day. They were themselves, were true to themselves, were unashamed of what they were and had, conducted themselves accordingly and were champions for God. Arising from that, we may say that the answer they received to their prayers was, "I, the Lord have placed you where you are for such a time as this, and you have all that you need for the demands of the hour. In the past you used competently and successfully all that you are and have, and that often for your own lawful ends; you need not behave differently now. Of course, I know the frailties of your flesh. There is sure to be tension and apprehension, but in the strength My grace supplies relax, be confident, be bold, and I will take care of the rest''. If that sounds like over simplification, remember that many Christians have gone through crises in a nerve torturing, stumbling, fumbling, grumbling manner because they were too tense to appreciate the relaxing power of faith. Others vainly imagined that the big crises demanded miraculous powers and superhuman effort, and they tried to win through as though they had such powers and could muster such strength, only to discover that they were beating the air in a dramatically absurd and useless manner. Or, knowing that they had not such powers and were incapable of such efforts, they gave up the fight before it had started and had to be dragged through the crisis complaining how ill done to they were. Life is a constant preparatory course for tomorrow and its needs, which we cannot see. Living naturally and using the faculties, talents and abilities we possess, we prove that they are sufficient for the demands of every day life, and practice and experience build up confidence and expertise in their use. Consequently, when the unusual is encountered and considered prayerfully, it is found that the resources are within ourselves to deal with the problem. When they are used in the strength of the Lord, the problem is solved. That is intelligent action in response to intelligent prayer. That is the providences of the Lord at work.

It was an important part of Esther's strategy to invite both the king and Haman to what would be called today a cocktail party (Esth.2:3-5). What to the two men seemed nothing more than an innocuous social occasion, which for the husband meant little more than pleasing his wife of whom he had been forgetful of late, and for the other a prestigious event (Esth.2:12), was designed by the queen that she might have these two arch conspirators confront each other as she impressed upon them the full implications of their dastardly plot. No doubt, she was hoping to convince the king that he had been deceived by a glib tongue and a specious bribe into doing irreparable damage to his kingdom, and that his love for her would sway the balance in favour of the Jews. That is precisely what happened (Esth.7:1-7). None can dispute Esther's astuteness, but it required a second wine party before the trap she had prepared was sprung (Esth.2:6-8). Did her nerve fail her on that first occasion when she saw how close these two men were, that she required another night of prayer and reflection to restore her courage? Or was it part of her scheme? I think the latter. The first party was exploratory, a testing of the ground. That the king was prepared to set aside matters of state by responding enthusiastically to her whim of having another get-together just for the three of them meant for her that he was in a frame of mind to do almost anything she asked; and, of course, Haman was completely disarmed by her coyness, left without defence when she struck. Every battle requires a general, and every general must know the terrain in which he fights, the foe he is confronting and the forces at his command; and he must use his knowledge so to deploy his troops in order to have his enemy at a disadvantage and to strike the deadly blow when and where it is least expected. That was Esther, that should be the Christian engaged in spiritual warfare. Conquering spiritual adversaries is not simply a matter of praying and then hoping that everything will be all right. God often answers our prayers by helping us to answer them for ourselves. If there is a weight which is hindering progress, be it human, physical or temporal, it must be discarded by him who carries it; if there is besetting sin, it must be got rid of by the person tormented by it (Heb.12:1). This requires thought, initiative, the deployment of talents and energies, the assistance of friends, persistence and courage. To say, ''I have not the will power or the determination'' is simply another way of saying, ''I do not want to conquer''. Faith prevails when, strengthened by prayer, it plans its tactics and acts accordingly.

Esther's plan was augmented by the Providence of God. Here it must be remarked that the workings of Providence cannot be anticipated, or if it is accepted that it is an ally, as it should be, it should be kept in mind that it usually works in ways not thought of by those concerned. Either it works secretly, making the campaign easier and victory inevitable, or so makes its movements obvious that the campaigner gladly avails himself of the opportunities it affords of triumphing. He who waits for Providence to work for him is generally disappointed. He who works and fights knowing that all things are working together for his good because called according to purpose, even though he cannot see how, will be in a position at the close of the day to recollect how this event and that circumstance, being in a certain place and meeting a particular person contributed to receiving the blessing he is currently experiencing, though maybe in a painful way. Paul, seeking to know where he should go next in the service of the gospel, thought of Asia but was brought to admit that meantime that was a prohibited place. He then attempted to enter Bithynia but found the way barred. Luke attributed these hindrances to the Holy Spirit, and so they were, but we are not told what means He used to prevent the apostle going to Asia or Bithynia. Later, Paul had a dream in which he saw and heard a Macedonian requesting help, and was convinced immediately that that was the place to which he should go (Acts 16:6-10). It led to the conversion of Lydia, the curing of a mentally deranged girl and, in consequence, to an unjust flogging and imprisonment. Despite the barbarity they were subjected to, Paul and his colleague prayed and sang praises at midnight. They praised because Providence had been at work to increase their glory and joy in the ministry (I Thess.2:20). And Providence continued to work, even as they sang, and in a miraculous manner which secured the conversion of their gaoler and his family. They then were released (Acts 16:12-40). None of that could be anticipated by them. They simply seized every opportunity to do what good they could, and Providence did the rest. Christians must endeavour as though all depended on them, and on them alone; so doing, sooner or later they will learn that Providence has been guiding their footsteps and directing their energies and working on their behalf, though sometimes apparently against them, and with them to achieve the Lord's designs.

Returning to Esther: we are permitted to see how, unbeknown to her, the Lord was working behind the scenes to make her defeat of Haman easier. First, there was the fly in the ointment of his success. His ecstacy at being invited along with the king to Esther's private party was dampened considerably by Mordecai's persistent refusal to honour him in the prescribed manner. It soured what was otherwise a sweet cup and agitated him (Esth.2:9-13). Then, on the eve of the second party, the king could not sleep. To while away the long, dark hours he perused the records of his reign. Maybe, he wanted to boost his ego, for sleeplessness can induce feelings of weakness, helplessness and frustration; and the reminder of what he had done to sustain and advance his kingdom might be what would do that for him. His eye lighted on how he had been preserved from the evil designs of Bigthan and Teresh by the timely information supplied by Mordecai, but no mention was made of any honour having been paid to this loyal servant. That had to be rectified at once. No life was more valuable than the king's, no security more important than his. Haman was not asleep that night either, but for a more fiendish reason. At his wife's and friends' suggestion he had been supervising the building of a scaffold from which to hang Mordecai, and so intense was his hatred he could not wait until the morning to secure the royal permission to execute his enemy. It was the haste of a man whose morale was ebbing fast, and how he grasped at the king's first words to him, "What shall be done to the man whom the king delights to honour?" as the fillip his dejected spirit needed. "Surely he was the only man the monarch would wish to invest with his favour!" Immediately he pigeon-holed Mordecai's execution. That could wait. He let his imagination run riot as there and then he devised a most extravagant procession, even by Eastern standards, in which he would be the sole focus of attention and which fell a trifle short of making him the equal of the king. His chagrin was indescribable when he was instructed to lavish all he had proposed upon Mordecai, his arch enemy. If his morale was low when he entered the royal bedchamber, it had hit rock bottom as he left. But Providence was not quite finished with him. Returning home, dejected and despairing, having perforce done to his bitterest enemy what he dearly wanted done to himself, he poured out all his woes into the ears of his household. Their response did not help him any. Rather unsympathetically he was informed that since his adversary was a Jew whose star was now on the ascendant, he could not hope to gain the upper hand. He was falling and would continue to fall until he was broken completely (Esth.6:13). It was with the heaviest of hearts and leaden feet that he went to Esther's second party, in no position to fend off any further attacks on his wounded pride, unprepared for and not expecting the exposure of his villiany. His demeanour and conduct before Esther's scathing condemnation was that of blind panic and hopeless despair which inevitably sealed his fate. Esther had prayed wisely and bravely, had acted intelligently and courageously and Providence did the rest.

Crisis is quite a common feature of the kingdom of God on earth and of individual Christians, but crises have come and gone, the kingdom remains and Christian have been kept by the power of God through faith unto salvation. When at such times there is a casting of ourselves and what concerns us on the mercy of God, a sincere facing up to the facts as we bow before Him, an earnest seeking for the wisdom which He gives liberally, and a determined effort to deal with the problem constructively and confidently, then Providence co-operates, then influences are brought to bear on the situation that the Lord might do for us exceeding abundantly above all we can either ask or think; and great is the relief and the rejoicing in the heart of the individual and of the Church when the Lord effects our deliverance.

ACCORDING TO PURPOSE
VII
THE VICTIM OF PROVIDENCE

Haman is one of a long line of individuals that has attempted the extermination of the Jews and/or the Church of Christ, the true Israel of God. Generally speaking, where the one is persecuted so also is the other, although political expediency and the like have meant that on occasion the one and not the other was attacked, as was the case when Nero vented his hatred on the Christians and not on the Jews. Beginning with "the king who knew not Joseph" (Ex.1:8), the line extends through Sennacherib, Nebuchadnezzar, Haman, Nero, Domitian and many more down to Hitler and Stalin. All in this unholy succession lie in the tomb, Israel remains and the Church continues. For many of those persecutors their end was as ignominious as the fate they had determined for their victims. For instance, Sennacherib was murdered by his own sons (II Kgs.19:37); Haman was executed, ironically on the gallows he himself had prepared for a Jew, by the king he had bribed to destroy the Jews (Esth.7:10); Nero was mad and died a violent death at his own command; Hitler committed suicide sitting amidst the ruins of his Third Reich, and Stalin, though he died still holding the reins of power, was discredited after his death by the very regime he had established in a most ruthless manner. "I will curse him that curses you" (Gen.12:3) is one of the most fearsome imprecations to come from the lips of God, a terrifying reminder that His word continues true to all generations and that He is the God Who does what He says.

What kind of man was Haman? Scripture is silent on his physical appearance, as it is on that of most of the characters with whom it concerns itself. Exceptions to that include Joseph (Gen.39:6), David (I Sam.16:12), Absalom (II Sam.14:25,26) and a few others whose looks had some bearing on the narrative. The Scriptures are more concerned with the heart of a man. It is that that makes a person what he really is (Matt.12:34,35 cf. 15:18,19). A man may be both an Adonis and a rascal, another may be as plain as a pikestaff, yet one of whom God and men approve. The body is but the box which holds the gems of grace and virtue or a receptacle encasing the evil smelling germs of vice and vanity. When the box is opened and the jewels scintillate, they and not the box attract attention and are commended; when like an opened Pandora's Box a person exudes evil influences, no one is impressed with his looks, though many might have been deceived for a time by them. Haman was an open Pandora's Box.

He was a man who belied his name. Haman means celebrated. It was the name given to a prince, one who by birth and privilege was likely to have a distinguished career in the service of his country, or to a son whose devoted parents had the social standing to hope great things for him and the wherewithal to fire his ambitions and open the doors to fame. If the Hebrew Haman is a cognate of the noun hamon, translated variously in the Old Testament as abundance, company, multitude, noise, riches, rumbling, store and tumult, it carries the thought of muchness or largeness, and can be understood in either a good or a bad sense. Where the sense is bad, a person can be considered celebrated in that he is notorious or infamous because he is known to be of ill-repute. That is how the Book of Esther presents Haman to the reader. A man of position and wealth, of intelligence and talent, influential, friendly and convivial where and when it suited him, single minded, self centred, unscrupulous in the pursuit of his goals, and a sycophant to boot. He was an individual who could skilfully manipulate others to bring his schemes to a successful climax, one not to be trusted at any price. Having said that, we find ourselves asking, ''Was he always that kind of person?'' That question is prompted by his failure to fulfil the high hopes of his parents when naming him Haman, and by what we see and know of him from this book during the last few weeks or months of his life (Esth.3; 5:9-14; 6:4-14; 7:1-10). We would like to think that at one time he had walked in more humane and constructive ways, but even if our charity is misplaced and it could be proved that the child was the father of the man, sufficient is known to permit us to say that he was the victim of Providence.

It might be argued that his parents were to blame for what Haman became. Without doubt, they were the first and the strongest formative force in his life and on his character; and perhaps they were influential in the wrong way. The light of their lives, the joy of their hearts, the morning star of their hopes, they could not fail to communicate to him what he meant to them and what they thought of him. By word and deed they gave to him an importance dangerous for any child to have; by their promptings and encouragements they gave the impression that no goal was beyond his reach, and that the path to it had been smoothed out for him. They tolerated his foibles as expressions of his genius, comforted him in his tantrums and gave him his own way; so much so, that, when away from his own home, he met with opposition and discovered to his amazement that he was not the centre of attraction everywhere. That made him all the more determined to have his own way wherever and whenever he could. In later life, when following his chosen career, his upbringing made him impervious to reasonable criticism, gave him the agility to side-step obstacles to obtaining his own ends, to proceed as though others and their opinions were of little or no significance, or to steam-roller over them as he progressed along his self appointed course. Is he more to be pitied than blamed? Not really. Life is a very hard school in which the teachers - those who are the scholar's equal, those who are superior to him in talent and brain power, the hard facts of life, particularly the sobering ones which reminded him that success is not automatic, that outsiders do not see as parents do, that the self confessed extraordinary person is really very ordinary - should cut the pupil down to size, that he might see himself as he really is and learn to readjust himself to live a healthy, normal life in co-operation with others. In this school Haman was a most obtuse scholar. He could not, would not bring himself to admit that his parents had exaggerated his potential and importance.

He was what he had been led to believe he was. His ego refused to be turned out of its course and to be satisfied unless he continued to prove to others in a most calculated manner that they were inferior and must occupy second place to him. In other words, he accepted his upbringing as his birthright and deliberately made himself what he considered himself to be, and what he became. Whatever blame might be apportioned to his parents, he himself was wholly responsible for the end result. Bearing in mind that he did not choose his parents nor they him, that his life was, as all life is, an act of God, it follows that the relationship which existed between them was of God. In brief, he was the fruit and victim of Providence.

Others might argue that Haman had fallen foul of hereditary traits. These are very real. They include the looks, the mannerisms, the abilities, the leanings and the charcteristics which contribute to the individual personality. Each child carries them from birth as part of his family inheritance, and in one way or another they help shape his life. Molly Lefebure writes, "Samuel Coleridge Taylor, in common with the rest of us, had no real choice in the matter of deciding who, and what, he was fundamentally to be. We none of us select for ourselves those mysterious congenital blueprints which we bring into the world as individuals, computer programmed pilot guides to our future, directions irrevocably built into each of us before we were expelled into orbit from the amniotic launch pad. Nor do we select the environment of our early shaping years" (Samuel Coleridge Taylor: A Bondage Of Opium, p.67). These tendencies are the outcome of the fusion of individual human streams by conception from three, four or more generations back. Each set of parents transmits to their child something of what they themselves have received from their progenitors, and each 'something' so intermingles in the child that the fusion becomes a special, a unique part of his make-up. A child may be seen to have the mannerisms of a grandparent or even a great grandparent whom he never saw or knew. His facial features when seen from one angle may reflect the likeness of a maternal aunt or uncle, and when seen in another light that of his father or other paternal relation. There has been a mixing of likenesses, one of which might predominate, to produce the individual personal appearance the child has. That of itself might be of little or no significance, but there are more serious and important aspects of heredity. A child may have a generous streak of nature or a very selfish one transmitted to him; he may shows signs of a leaning toward a particular activity or habit, good or bad, which can be traced back to some forebear or is a characteristic of one of the families from which he has sprung. Not for the first time has it been said, when a young person has expressed himself in a particular way or shown a bias toward some special activity, "Well, what do you expect? Look who his father is!" or "That's not surprising; that poor creature has bad blood in him!" Heredity is a fact of life which all accept, but when men say of another that he has bad blood in him, are they excusing or condemning him for his conduct? Some in the softness of their hearts might pity, but the law of the land and the majority of his fellows hold him responsible and judge him guilty. Invariably, what a person is, whatever he might have inherited from the past, he has made himself. "No man", says Goethe, "is responsible for his heredity until he has made it his own". He who comes from a family background with a reputation for charity and generosity may prove himself to be a selfish wretch; he whose antecedents were drunkenness and gambling by his sobriety and careful, thrifty use of his resources might be the odd one out in the family circle. In either case, the person concerned knows that he is not acting from uncontrollable compulsion, knows what he is about, can give reasons why he wants to behave as he does. So it was with Haman. The worst of blood might have flowed in his veins, but he was his own man, the man he wanted to be, bent on achieving the ends on which he had set his sights and in the manner most suitable to himself. None could accuse him of not being deliberate and responsible. But since God has so created man that this transmission of good or bad to one's offspring is inevitable and part of the unity of the human race, it can be said that what Haman was, as well as how, when and where he was born, and the part he played in the purpose of God, made him the victim of Providence.

The phrase 'victim of Providence' might sound harsh and sinister, but it is true because Haman made it so. He was his own victim. He was a very talented man, had sufficient gifts to make a success of life, every one of which was from God. He was favoured by Providence though he neither knew nor acknowledged God. The gifts of God are inherently good and are without repentance. They are given to permit the receiver to contribute to the sum total of goodness in the world. It is the responsibility of the receiver to use them to that end. If the responsibility is shunned and the user perverts and misdirects his talents to gratify his own selfish ambitions or lusts, he is adding to the wickedness, misery and sadness which are prevalent everywhere. What was intended to be constructive is used destructively, but the destruction begins in the heart of the user. He who uses the good gifts of God for the well being of others increases his own sense of well being, but he who misdirects them for personal gain alone has in effect made them incapable of good work, and they destroy what he plans to create, his own good. Absalom, David's son was handsome, charming and a born leader, gifts which could have contributed much to the prosperity of Israel had he been content to act as his father's aide. But, desiring the kingdom for himself and the gratification of his pride, he chose to use his talents to create strife in the land and to turn the people from his father, the Lord's anointed, to himself. His rebellion caused much hardship and misery and many deaths, and brought about his own destruction. The same fate overtook Haman and for the same reasons. He was too gifted for his own good. His talents assured success and made life easy for him. As advance after advance attended him, he became convinced that whatever he contrived would be accomplished, that he was unstoppable. That was his undoing. His misdirected use of his skills led him blindly to a precipice and to one ill-judged step which took him over the top.

Placing divine providence and human responsibility side by side without making any attempt to reconcile them, and thereby implying perhaps that they are irreconcileable, might give rise to the charge that God is unfair. He has made man as he is, makes no attempt to prevent him taking the wrong course of action, but rather by this thing called Providence exploits the weaknesses of men to achieve His own ends. It is a criticism which usually comes from those who, when they hear of sovereign grace in salvation with its emphasis on election and predestination as well as faith, complain that we are denying man free will, are making him an automaton or puppet. Whether it be with reference to salvation or personal conduct man is responsible. With regard to his use of his talents and faculties and the performing of his proper function in life, God has given to man a special capacity, namely, the ability to be tempted. Temptation itself is not evil. If it were, the Lord Jesus could not be sinless, for He was tempted and tried in all points like as we are, sin excepted (Heb.2:18; 4:15). Basically, temptation is testing in order to prove the stability and trustworthiness of an individual and has a disciplinary value. He who passes the test has not only demonstrated his commitment to a particular business but has strengthened himself to pass future tests as they arise, and so makes himself more resolute and capable in the performance of what has been entrusted to him. Temptation has its source within the individual, is latent within him because of what God has given him to do. Temptation or the awareness of temptation was inbuilt into man created in the image of God, and by reason of the authority and power invested in him by God. Created to be God's viceregent on the earth, to be underlord of the earth and its content and answerable to God, his position was a very onerous one. He could not do what he pleased but must please God at all times. He was free to please God, and that called for the diligent use of his talents and faculties. He was at liberty to think best how to discharge his office, subject to any restriction placed upon him by God. Within that freedom lay the possibility of temptation, which exposed his trustworthiness to testing. It is not an attempt to excuse Adam's conduct when we say that, when thinking how best he could do his job, the thought struck him that knowing good and evil, as opposed to knowing only good, would be an advantage to him. The possibility of knowing was there to hand, and it was what an honest, conscientious workman would think, but it should have been dismissed immediately as forbidden by the Lord. However, he permitted the thought to persist until it became so strong, so obsessive, it passed from thought to desire, became compulsive in its urge. The initial thought was not wrong, but the desire it conceived was (cf.Jas.1:13-15). The man failed because he did not bring the thought of being a better workman for God into the light of God's requirement. Had he done so, the thought would have been rejected and he made a stronger workman. We see that illustrated in the wilderness temptations of Jesus (Matt.4:1-11). His God appointed business was to attract men to Himself (cf.John 12:32) in order to reconcile them to God, and to found the kingdom of God on the earth (cf. Matt.16:18). His thought was, "How best can this be accomplished? and can it be attained if I, having the power to sustain myself, starve?" That thought and the suggestions it evoked of quick and easy ways of drawing men to himself and acquiring authority over the nations of the world He considered in the light of the commission He had received. Immediately He perceived that they were not in accord with God's mind and rejected them as being of the devil. That was His reasoning in Gethsemane also. Holiness of life and communion with His God and Father were precious to Him; so precious, that the thought of being made sin and forsaken, even temporarily, by His God were repugnant to Him, pressed heavily upon His spirit, demanding that another way of saving mankind be found. But the thought was not permitted to become a desire that controlled Him. He reacted strongly against it, praying in a most strenuous manner, "O my Father, if it is possible, let this cup pass from me; nevertheless, not my will but thine be done". So great was the pressure, the thought persisted, to be countered again by an even more determined supplication, "O my Father, if this cup pass not away from me except I drink it, thy will be done". So horrifying was the awareness of what being made sin for us meant to Him personally, that it required a third and similar plea, so physically and mentally distressing in its fervency, that it caused a great sweating of blood to pour down His face; but on that third occasion the thought died completely and He was resolved that cost what it would, it would be His delight to do His Father's will (Matt.26:36-46). From that moment and until He commended His spirit into His Father's hands He was impervious to all temptation. Such thoughts as Adam and Jesus had, and all men have, are not sinful; but they become so when they expel all else from the mind except that of gratifying self interest, and give rise to conduct contrary to truth and righteousness.

Unlike the Lord Jesus Haman had forfeited both the experience and the blessing of temptation. It was a boon he had had in common with all men but it had been so mishandled and abused by him that it ceased to have a place either in his vocabulary or philosophy of life. Where others said, "I was tempted," his response was, "I had an idea". That is, the thought that he had was not seen as a warning signal, an amber light indicating that he should proceed with caution until convinced that it was right and proper to travel a particular way; he saw it not as a red light commanding him to stop when the path diverged before him, and to deliberate and seek advice on which was the right way to choose. He was not concerned whether his thought was right or wrong in moral terms but with how it could best benefit himself and advance his plans for his own aggrandisement. If, on reflection, the idea was seen to be impractical, it was discarded; but if considered worthwhile, it was adopted with zest, irrespective of what it might mean for others. To all intents and purposes it was a system which worked, as it seems to have done and is doing for many others like him. In the words of the Psalmist, Haman "was not in trouble as other men, neither was he plagued like other men" (Ps.73:5). He walked a plain path of unhindered progress, success came easy to him, he had the midas touch, gave to his family every conceivable comfort and luxury, and amassed a fortune to leave as a legacy to his children. But a railway track without signals is a very dangerous line to travel. It might be clear of obstacles but where is it leading? Without signals it is not intended for use and its terminus not a desirable one. It cannot be said to lead nowhere, for there is no such place. These were the Psalmist's conclusions when he viewed this track in the light of God's revelation. Annoyed that such as Haman should have a comfortable, trouble free ride, he went into the house of God, perhaps to complain as did Job before him and Jeremiah at a later date, but there he saw light in God's light. He confessed, "Then understood I their end" (Ps.73:17). He saw a line not only barren of signals but one on which such brakes as the traveller had were ineffective, a track which did not go on indefinitely. He saw the complacent traveller enjoying his ride, then suddenly there was no track, no means of stopping, just a great bog which sucked its screaming, hapless victim into the depths of destruction. "There is a way which seems right to a man, but the end thereof are the ways of death" (Prov.14:12).

A great tragedy, yet the Providence of God. One would shrink from thinking in this vein were it without the warrant of Scripture, but the testimony of the Word of God to it is so clear as not to be gainsaid. Four examples spring readily to mind. First, there is Pharaoh. He boasted of absolute power, considered the unseen God of Israel as impotent as a chunk of rock, and his own plans for the Jews inviolate. After all, had he not done with them as he wished for many a long year without being resisted or thwarted by anyone! But God said to this king who delighted in defying Him, "In very deed, for this cause have I raised thee up, for to shew in thee my power, and that my name might be declared throughout the whole earth"(Ex.9:16). Subsequent events proved that to be true. Then there was Sihon, king of Heshbon. He refused to grant the children of Israel free passage through his land, even though they undertook not to use any of the country's resources for their sustenance. Rather, Sihon attacked the Israelites and was humiliatingly defeated for his pains. Later, when reviewing the journeyings of Israel and the goodness of God to them, Moses had this to say of Sihon, "Sihon, king of Heshbon would not let us pass by him: for the Lord thy God hardened his spirit, and made his heart obstinate, that he might deliver him into thy hand, as appeareth this day. And the Lord said unto me, Behold, I have begun to give Sihon and his land before thee: begin to possess, that thou mayest begin to inherit his land" (Deut.2:30,31). Moving on to the two sons of Eli, Hophni and Phineas, priests of God, but described as "sons of Belial, they know not the Lord" (I Sam.2:12). They despised their office, made a mockery of worship and caused others to abhor it. Eli reasoned and remonstrated with them but "they hearkened not unto the voice of their father, because the Lord would slay them" (I Sam.2:25). Then, finally, there was Saul, the man whom God appointed to be king of Israel when the people, rejecting Him as their unseen head, demanded an ordinary monarch as had other nations. As a king Saul was a disaster. He was the expression of God's judgment on the nation for their dismissal of Him. Speaking through Hosea, and obviously referring to Saul's reign, the Lord said, "I gave thee a king in mine anger, and took him away in my wrath"

(Hos.13:11). Each of these characters was either inhumane, sacrilegious or foolish. They were destroyed. They were brought to judgment by the God Whose people and purpose they were damaging by their conduct. It was part of His purpose to do so; yet slowly, systematically, if somewhat blindly, they accomplished their own ruin. God left them alone but overruled what they were and did. As such, they were the victims of Providence.

Alongside these victims there are the beneficiaries of Providence, the Esthers, the Mordecais and the rank and file of the kingdom of God. The targets of men's wrath and foolishness, they are the objects of God's grace, those in and through whom He will be glorified throughout an ageless eternity. What men meant for ill God used for good. For much of the time it seemed that those whom God had covenanted to bless were the victims of a harsh, bitter or cruel Providence, while their enemies and those indifferent to God benefitted from a kind and gentle Providence; but if all these adjectives be dropped, and Providence likened to electricity, it becomes evident that the apparatus to which it is connected determines its effects. For instance, if attached to a light bulb, electricity gives light; if joined to a fire, it emits heat, to a motor it produces motion; but if connected to a refrigerator or freezer, it creates coldness and hardness. Similarly with the Providence of God: to him to whom the Spirit of God has given a new heart Providence engenders love and understanding, confidence and trust, submission and hope in relation to God. Convinced that "God is too wise to err, too loving to be unkind" the redeemed soul responds positively, if sometimes tearfully and painfully, to the workings of God, believing that the ends God has in mind always justify His means. Whereas, he who has no heart for God takes the good that comes his way as a matter of course and as his right, and grows increasingly indifferent to the God Who provides; and when hardship comes his way, as it does to all sooner or later, he develops the rigid stoicism of the individual who imagines that he is able to cope with whatever strikes him, or who sinks into a deep cavern of bitterness from which to complain that the goodness of God is a travesty of the truth. The victim of Providence.

ACCORDING TO PURPOSE
VIII
THE DAY THE LORD MADE

The 13th of Adar - that is, the lunar month extending from the new moon in March to the one in April - in the twelfth year of the reign of Ahasuerus was a fateful day for the Persian Empire. Then the anti-Semitists hoped to have a field day.Thanks to the arch-conspirator, Haman, and a foolish decree from the king they could massacre every Jew in the kingdom and that without let or hindrance. They relished the prospect, made their plans, prepared and stored their weapons carefully, while the more sadistic among them devised devilish schemes to increase the Jews' sufferings and their own pleasure. As news of the preparations leaked out and became more macabre with the telling, the terror of the Jews increased. For them there was no escape, no place for them to hide. Who can tell the sleepless nights many of these hapless Israelites endured, the minds that snapped under the strain forcing them into the life beyond the grave through the forbidden door, the tears which soaked many pillows, the heartrending prayers which pierced the silence of darkened bedrooms as week after week slow painful day followed long torturous night. Intentionally or otherwise, the lengthy period between issuing the decree and its planned execution, while a mercy of Providence, did add considerably to the Jews' tribulation. As the rest of the Empire followed their daily pursuits, thoughtful, sympathetic, apprehensive but powerless to assist the Jews in their plight, the burden of loneliness, forsakenness, hopelessness weighed down with ever increasing heaviness upon the shoulders of the Hebrews. But there was an Eye that never sleeps, an Ear that was not deaf to their groanings and pleadings, an Arm that was not shortened that it could not save. Though the majority of the Jews were unaware of it, God had bottled their tears, recorded their groanings in His book of remembrance. He had not forgotten His people. He had prepared Himself to take action. The 13th day of Adar would be a momentous one. It was the day the Lord had made.

The 13th of Adar was a day determined by Providence. We have seen already that the superstition of the age dictated, by the casting of dice, that that was the most appropriate date for what Haman had in mind. But God had control of the dice. Hamon breathed on them and flung them, but God rolled them to a time eleven months hence. Haman was quite content - God had set His time. The dice had spoken - God had ordained. Haman and the Lord were both agreed on that date and both prepared themselves for the events of the day; but there the agreement ends. Haman had his plans, but they were diametrically opposed to God's purpose. Haman had the destruction of the Jews in mind; God was concerned with the preservation of Israel and His judgment on His enemies. Either, but not both, of these events would take place on that far off day. Moreover, the date was fixed irrevocably. Haman would not, even if he could, change it. He did not believe for one moment that the dice could lie and so had no desire for change; but that apart, once the decree had been issued by the king the matter passed from his control. No decree emerging from the palace could be altered (Esth.8:8). Haman let chance determine a day, God fixed a date. That is a distinction with a difference. Haman anticipated what would happen and planned accordingly, God knew what would happen, for then He would act without fail. That was a truth the Pharisees like Haman learned the hard way. Jesus knew that the times which concerned Him were in His Father's hand, that the Father had appointed a place and manner and season of His death. He knew also that neither of these could be altered, and exactly where, how and when His Father's will would be executed. He spoke confidently of His hour, knew it could neither be brought forward nor postponed, and when it had come. The Pharisees in their ignorance and arrogance tried to interfere with God's timing. When they decided that Jesus should be arrested and put to death, they decreed, "Not on the feast day, lest there be an uproar among the people". At the very time the Sanhedrin was making these decisions Jesus said to His disciples, "Ye know that after two days is the Feast of the Passover, and the Son of man is betrayed to be crucified" (Matt.26:1-5). That feast day was God's appointed time when the Lamb of God should be sacrificed to inaugurate the New Testament Passover. It was then Jesus was crucified. It was the day the Lord had made.

The wisdom of this fixed interval of time is apparent. Without it the Book of Esther would not have been written, the history of the Jews would have come to an abrupt end, no foundation stone would be laid in Zion, the gates of hell had prevailed against the Church without the latter ever having been. How different the history of mankind. No Good Friday, no Easter Sunday. Without the possibility of refuge and deliverance from evil without and within, no promise of a changed, new life, no comfort in the sorrows and bereavements of life, no hope of life beyond the grave, only a great nameless dread as death approached or was contemplated. Without these days would mankind have survived? Doubtful. Despite the preserving power of the gospel life (Matt.2:13), a force which has made life palatable for many peoples and generations, the corruption which is in the world through lust seems to increase, and evil men more audacious in their scheming and perpetrating of wickedness. Had there been no gospel influence, no righteous force at work through the children of God the world must have perished long since in a welter of corruption. But God did intervene. There was a 13th of Adar, a Good Friday, an Easter Day, a Pentecost, days when, a short time before all seemed lost, the Lord strong and mighty went forth conquering and to conquer. They were days when the expectations of the enemies of God and His covenant were thwarted, when the guilt of sin against the Lord's people was cancelled out, and their accuser silenced; when death, the last enemy His people meet, was left behind, buried in the tomb when the risen Lord left it. That tomb was left open. Jesus' disciples could move in and out of it without fear, symbolic of their deliverance from the fear of death. These were the days also when the redeemed of the Lord received power so to live that sin would no longer have dominion over them, when the living Christ would indwell them, they have the ability to put off the old man or life and put on Christ or the new life in Him. So equipped they walk in newness of life, looking for the blessed hope and glorious appearing of the Lord Jesus Christ, when they will be forever with Him. Truly, "the days the Lord made; we rejoice and are glad in them" (Ps.118:24).

The 13th of Adar was a fateful day for the enemies of the Jews. How quickly a day can change. The calm brightness of morning often gives way to the stormy darkness of early afternoon and evening. What begins with exuberant confidence ends in gloomy tragedy; but the real tragedy is that the victims of the tragedy were deceived by the clear warm dawn and were unaware, or took no notice, of portents in the new day which signalled its dismal ending. Often, a novice yachtsman and his crew set sail lured by a promising morning and a calm sea, without consulting weather forecasts or the advice of those experienced in the ways of weather and ocean. And there was moaning at the bar when they did not return from the sea. That long Persian day which stretched from the first to the twelfth month underwent dramatic changes in its political climate, changes which left Haman, captain of the yacht dead, and his craft and crew, including his sons foundering in mountainous seas which swept them on to the rocks of God's vengeance, where they were destroyed. It was a day they did not live to remember but one which they do not forget throughout a God-less eternity. Had they been cognisant of the signs contained in the Word of God and history the tragedy need not have happened; but it did because they were ignorantly confident of their own prowess to tackle efficiently what time and circumstance might throw at them.

Having earlier dealt somewhat with the signs which heralded the storm about to overtake Haman and his confederates, we concentrate here on the events of the 13th and 14th of Adar. Before doing so, we must bear in mind that we are dealing with a state of civilisation which by and large was vastly different from our own. The events recorded in Esther chapter 9 were typical of that day and age and must be seen in that context. The Jews with the law of Moses in their hands and hearts did not consider they were violating any part of it acting as they did. On the contrary, the opportunity to defend themselves and destroy their enemies they knew to be an act of God, an answer to prayer when they least expected it. It would have been sinful as well as self defeating to have acted otherwise. That day was one when they must destroy or be destroyed. There was no other alternative. It must not be overlooked that even though these Israelites had been given permission to defend themselves, the decree demanding the killing of every man, woman and child of them still stood. Nor was it simply a matter of saving their own lives at the expense of others, but of preserving a God given heritage, way of life and faith vital not only to that generation of Jews but to their children, their children's children and to the world. Nor was it blood lust, a relish for killing and a desire for gain that made them defend themselves with the enthusiasm they did. Wherever they fought, either in the capital or the provinces, "they laid not their hands on the prey" (Esth.9:15,16). They killed no innocent person, they looted no man's property, they purloined no other's goods. How many modern armies can make that boast? Defending themselves, they fought according to the precepts of the law of Moses. They committed no murder, they did not steal, nor did they covet another's possessions. They fought a righteous war righteously. Nor did the non-Jews who considered the king's first decree irreprehensible, and had sympathy and support for the Hebrews, view the behaviour of their friends as either excessive or inhuman.

That aside, Esther chapter 9 is part of the all scripture which is God-breathed and written for our profit (II Tim.3:16). There are lessons here which the Church, as the army of the Lord, must learn and practise. Like Mordecai and his compatriots we must at all times defend ourselves by using the opportunities Providence gives to attack. If we do not, the Church perishes, for she is under constant threat from the forces of evil. But our mission is not concerned with the annihilation of men but with their deliverance from evil, not the pursuit of monetary gain but the salvation of souls.

Our warfare is fought by those who are armed with the sword of the Spirit, which is the word of God (Eph.6:17f), and who are strengthened with prayer and made robust by the quality of life faith in Christ produces. Our battles are fought in the realms of human thought and conduct and against the superstitions and ignorance which are the fruit of sin, and against the philosophies which aim to destroy the truth by which we live and for which we stand. The vastness, the subtlety and the might of the forces opposing the Church are best summed up in the words of the apostle Paul: "We wrestle not against flesh and blood, but against principalities, against powers, against the rulers of the darkness of this world, against spiritual wickedness in high places" (Eph.6:12). That description conjures up the picture of an army whose strength, malignancy and malevolence can scarcely be exaggerated, whose antagonism is continuous with time, and which cannot be defeated by bombs and bullets however terrifying their destructive ability. Rather, to use such weaponry is to assist this evil force in its work. "The weapons of our warfare are not carnal", says Paul, "but mighty through God to the pulling down of strongholds" (II Cor.10:4). We make war as those who are made strong by truth, whose hearts are governed and protected by righteousness, who are ever ready to follow after peace with all men, the peace purchased with the blood of the cross, who live by faith, knowing that faith is the victory which overcomes the world, and whose minds are encased in the mighty fact of God's salvation, the salvation which cannot be destroyed, refuted or denied, and which is able to conquer and bring its stoutest opponents under its banner (cf. Eph.6:13-17). So equipped, and holding forth the word of life the Church is invincible, goes forward steadily from triumph to triumph. Many consider it a futile way to wage a war. If it is seen as one of ideas and ideals, the weight of learning and appeal seems to be with our opponents - the preaching of the cross is foolishness to them that are perishing (I Cor.1:18) - and their reasoning and logic seem to prevail; so much so, many on the Christian side attempt to accommodate what the Church most surely believes within the framework of the world's thinking, so weakening its striking force. This applies particularly to such articles of faith as the virgin birth and resurrection of Jesus Christ. Many liberal theologians claim to accept these facts but their explanation and defence of them are often illogical in the extreme, a vain attempt to decipher divine revelation in terms of subtle reasoning which fools none but those who have blinkered themselves to the truth. If, as has often happened, the Church's opponents resort to physical violence, what chance has its forces and principles in the face of last resort tactics of violence, imprisonments and murder? None it would seem, but this is the miracle of the Church: philosophies have come and gone because the grace and truth of the gospel have silenced them; armed force has sent many saints to a martyr's crown, but at the same time has replenished what it took away with new recruits from its own ranks. It was a strange but true report which one gave to Archbishop Beaton when Patrick Hamilton was martyred. "My lord", said his informant, "if ye shall burn them, let them be burned in deep cellars, for the reek of Master Patrick Hamilton has infected as many as it blew upon". And a most wonderful prophecy, soon to be fulfilled, came from the lips of Latimer and with which he encouraged his fellow sufferer, Ridley, being burned at the stake with him: "Be of good comfort, Master Ridley, and play the man. We shall this day light such a candle by God's grace in England, as I trust shall never be put out". Both these murders together with many more helped speed the advance of gospel truth in Scotland and England. Then, as in the days of the apostles, and as now, the world made determined attempts to remove the Church by one means or another; but then, as now, it was, and still is the day which the Lord has made for the spread and triumph of the gospel. He says, "Behold, now is the accepted time; behold, now is the day of salvation" (II Cor.6:2). Still we can say with Paul, "The things which have happened unto us have fallen out rather for the furtherance of the gospel" (Philp.1:12). Therefore, let us be glad and rejoice in this day, ever fighting the good fight of faith manfully, praying as we do, "Save now, we beseech thee, send now prosperity" (Ps.118:24,25).

Another lesson we may learn from the Jews on that day fatal to the schemes of those that conspired against them was their thoroughness. They left none alive that was opposed to them (Esth.9:5). The scene appears barbaric to our eyes, but before attempting an explanation and vindication of this slaughter, let us ask ourselves, "Has the conduct of civilised nations changed much in this respect since Old Testament times?" It has not. The mass murder of millions of Jews by Hitler, the extermination of millions more together with millions of Russians purged by Stalin, the cruelty the Japanese meted out to prisoners of war and to their own wounded in Burmah and elsewhere during the 1940s equals, if not exceeds, the atrocities of former, less sophisticated times. Nor are we as a nation excluded from this comparison. We cannot condemn what the Jews did under Mordecai and excuse the ruthless pursuit of the unconditional surrender of the Nazis and the dropping of an atomic bomb on Hiroshima. Nearer our own day and place, the hate inspired determination of certain trade union leaders to crush all opposition to their designs, irrespective of who gets hurt and however badly, and the vindictiveness of strikers against non-striking colleagues, threatening their lives and property or with permanent ostracism because they refuse to collaborate; and the senseless slaughter of lives and destruction of property indulged in by para-military organisations in the pursuit of a political ideal are as inhuman as anything claimed to be found in the Bible. Those concerned bristle with indignation when condemned for their policies and actions, not considering that they are doing wrong. Their attitude justifies us asking as we consider the thoroughness of the Jews when defending their lives and homes, "Was there not cause or reason?"

The slaughter under Mordecai was not uncommon in the history of Israel or in Biblical times. The complete destruction of their enemies, particularly of those whom they ousted from the Promised Land, almost had the force of a standing order from Jehovah, so often did He demand it (Deut.7:1,2,23,24; 20:16-18; Josh.6:24 etc.). Saul was dethroned by God because he refused to carry out such an order (I Sam.26:2,3,26). The Psalmist, aware that this was the policy of the Lord, prophesied a similar fate for Babylon as had overtaken other nations opposed to God's people (Ps.137:8), and then he adds these words, "Happy shall he be that taketh and dasheth thy little ones against the stones" (v.9). Such words cause many to shudder. So non-christian do they sound that one congregation the writer knows which uses the Psalms for responsive reading have omitted Psalm 137. The membership is convinced that such a sentiment is wrong. But that is to misunderstand the reason for the order. The Jewish love of children and the tenor of their faith as dictated by the moral law to love their neighbours as themselves, to humanely treat strangers and enemies and to regard human life as sacred caused them to shrink from indiscriminate and needless acts of human destruction just as we do. That the Lord expected and respected; therefore, when ordering the complete destruction of particular peoples, He was careful always to give reasons. The fearful sounding orders to annihilate the tribes and communities occupying the Promised Land, and who, as we have seen already, were so ingrained in evil ways and practices as to be beyond hope of reformation, was to prevent the Israelites from entering into a pact with them, and to remove the possibility of the Jews being tainted with idolatrous worship and corrupt practices which even in those far off days were too evil to contemplate (Ex.34:12-17). The destruction of heathen temples and images meant the removal of a strong temptation to follow a false religion and way of life (Deut.12:2). The proneness of Israel to idolatory made such an edict inevitable. The removal of the former inhabitants from Canaan was to prevent them teaching doctrines and practices abnoxious to God, and the destruction of their children a safeguard against the evils being continued by, and perpetuated in, them (Deut.20:16-18). This order from the throne of holiness was intended to keep a moral, terminal cancer from the body spiritual. That the Israelites failed to comply with this order was a direct cause of all the evil which contaminated the Jews and led ultimately to their being exiled from Canaan. In a similar way the thoroughness with which the Jews set on their enemies in the Persian Empire must be viewed. It was not only their enemies' or their own security that was at stake but the future of the covenant and the seed of Abraham. Also, there was the resolve to set a warning to all their potential enemies within the Empire. The Jews' ferocity and thoroughness were saying in effect, "When planning mischief against us, remember Haman and his collaborators". Esther's request that the slaughter be continued for a second day in Shushan and that the bodies of Haman's sons be hanged on public display has been criticised as being viciously vindictive and intolerable (Esth.9:12-15). It would be so today, but it was Esther's way of saying to all the king's subjects, "Beware the vengeance of Jehovah." Had Hitler and Stalin remembered to beware, the recent history of Europe might be vastly different. The Allies' policy of unconditional surrender demanded of Germany toward the end of the Second World War was designed as a deterrent to future aggressor nations with ambitions to be power supreme in the world. It was a policy which resulted in thousands of civilian casualties including many of the young. It was costly in the extreme but deemed necessary, if the nations were to get the message that aggression does not pay. But will they? If the constant resurgence of anti-Semitism and desire for world domination are criteria, the nations will never learn. Nevertheless, they have been warned and are without excuse.

Unfortunately, neither does the Church profit from the chastisements of the past. It is its business to keep itself unspotted from the world (Jas.1:17). Purity of doctrine, purity of worship, purity of life is the threefold demand Christ makes of His Church, seen repeatedly in the New Testament. The three parts of the demand are inter-related. Soil one and the other two are dirtied. Without a sincere desire to conform the life to New Testament standards, there can be no worship acceptable to God, no deep rooted understanding of the truths of the gospel; without that understanding or desire for it, there will be a lax approach to worship and a falling short of the exacting requirements for spiritual living; where there is no true reverence for God, there cannot be respect for His truth nor for His demands on the life. That might sound rather negative, but the New Testament's approach to the Church is identical to that of the Old Testament's to Israel. In the former as in the latter there are persistent warnings against idolatry and its pernicious effects on the membership. It is the antithesis of the worship and service of the God and Father of our Lord Jesus Christ. It is the progenitor of all that is evil and disgusting in the sight of God and consigns to the lowest levels of corruption wherever it reigns. The Church at Laodicea is a case in point (Rev.3:14-22). Therefore, the Temple or Church of God must have nothing whatever to do with idols (cf. II Cor.6:16). The membership has professedly turned to God from idols, to serve the living and true God (I Thess.1:9), and can do so only as idols are kept out. It is not possible to serve God and mammon. It must be one or the other (Matt.6:24). But the Church is not immune to this evil. It can infiltrate into the fellowship, and in the most insidious of ways. It might not be brought in in the crude form of an image or statue before which the congregation prostrates itself, but can enter as covetousness (Eph.5:5; Col.3:5). To covet is to lust after something, concrete or abstract, is to set it up in the heart as the one thing needful, convinced that to have it is to have all that is wanted. Unfortunately, should the lust be satisfied in one particular, another object quickly takes its place. Covetousness is the god that never says, ''I've had enough''. Covetousness reigns where Christians have not found their all in God. It breeds dissatisfaction with the worship and fellowship of the congregation, is prepared to tolerate what is extraneous and harmful to the spiritual life. Where it exists the witness of the congregation loses all power. In consequence, we are commanded to flee from covetousness as from a dangerous plague (I Cor.10:14), and to be quick to purge the congregation of it should it rear its ugly head there. Advocating this, Paul uses the strongest possible language. He writes, ''Now I am writing to you that you must not associate with anyone that calls himself a brother but is . . . greedy, an idolater . . . With such a man do not even eat'' (I Cor.5:11, N.I.V.). Discipline must be exercised to the point of separating from or excommunicating the offending party. This should be done in such a way that, if possible, the person concerned will be brought to repentance and the fellowship purged. Lack of discipline is the bane of the present day Church. Perhaps in the past it was ministered in a harsh, uncharitable, pharasaic manner, but that is no excuse for neglecting it. Where there is no proper exercise of discipline, there there is licence to be and do all that is dishonouring to God, and the Church reduced to what Israel was prior to the Exile, no different from the world. To safeguard against that we must be firm but compassionate, strict but loving, and must never make any compromise to evil, or deviate from the New Testament way of church life. With words of grace seasoned with salt we must enforce the apostolic injunction, ''Little children, keep yourselves from idols'' (I John 5:21). So doing, we shall be separate, touching not the unclean thing, and will hear the Almight say, ''I will receive you, and will be unto you a Father, and ye shall be my sons and daughters'' (II Cor.6:17,18).

Vengeance, the vengeance of the Lord, having been visited on their enemies, the Jews, as instructed by Mordecai, kept festival on the 14th and 15th Adar, dates he decreed should be included in the Jewish calendar of religious celebrations in perpetuity (Esth.9:18-23). This is a further instance of Mordecai's faith. he was confident that Israel, though at that time a subject people, would be re-established in their own land and for a long time to come; in fact, until Emmanuel came to ransom captive Israel. The experiences of the past eleven months convinced him of that. The God Who had brought His people out from the living death of Egypt with a mighty hand, had with the same hand gloved in gracious providences quite literally brought them back from the brink of the grave. Such displays of grace could mean but one thing, ''no weapon formed against them could prosper''. History and Providence had linked arms to prove it, and to give assurance respecting the future that none of God's words would fall to the ground.

The 13th of Adar was a triumphant, joyful occasion because it was "the day which the Lord had made". The Jews would have been the most unnatural and ungracious of nations had they not celebrated this victory. No nation or tribe has ever conquered its foes and not gone into ecstacies of delight and enjoyment. But those excited Israelites knew, as their fathers had known before them, that the battle had not been theirs but the Lord's. It was He and no other Who had appointed the day and prepared the field, and that victory had come to them not by their own might or power but by the Spirit of the Lord (Zech.4:6). That was the reason why they were glad and rejoiced. For them it was a resurrection day, a day when they ceased, momentarily at least, weeping by the rivers of Babylon, a day when the sound of the harp and psalms of praise to Jehovah were heard in the foreign land. The Lord Himself had turned their captivity, and though it seemed to many of them like a dream, so good was it it seemed scarcely true, yet their mouths were filled with laughter and their voices with singing. The day was real, the victory was real. There were their neighbours, people who did not know the Lord, standing applauding and shouting, "The Lord hath done great things for them, whereof they are glad". They need not pinch themselves any more to make sure it was no mirage. The Lord had stood by them, had strengthened them with all might in the inner man, and they could testify gladly, "The Lord hath done great things for us, whereof we are glad" (Pss. 137 & 126).

The 14th and 15th of Adar are the Christmas and Boxing Days of the Old Testament. What we read in Esther chapter 9, verse 22 is our warrant for saying that. It could be that with the passing of the years the occasion deteriorated into a riot of commercialism and entertainment which obliterated its true significance; nonetheless, it was a God sanctioned festival, and for many who waited for the consolation of Israel it would be a stimulus to faith and hope. They rejoiced, they celebrated because the deliverances of the past were heralds of the ultimate deliverance when Messiah came in the fulness of time. And they were keen that others should share the blessedness which was theirs. As they joined hands with like minded friends and relations around the festive board, how real and precious "the communion of saints, the hope of glory, and the life everlasting." As they remembered the poor, those who had nothing to celebrate with and perhaps felt they had nothing to celebrate, they would communicate something of the faith and hope which filled them and of the blessedness they were enjoying. As empty hands and stomachs were filled, and cheer came to chase the gloom, the love of the givers, and the present easing of poverty, however temporary, would come as a deliverance of grace to many, stir their memories to recall the bygone faithfulness of the Lord to His people, and would revive their flagging faith and hope, encouraging them to continue in the ways of God's promises. Christmas should be no less, and certainly much more, to us. Its inception was a most joyous occasion despite the gross darkness which enveloped the world and the man-made violence and misery which followed it. Was it not a moment of supreme happiness for Mary? The birth pangs behind her, her body at ease and her Child asleep in His manger, we can picture her again singing the Magnificat, but this time in duet with Jospeh, "My soul doth magnify the Lord, and my spirit rejoices in God my Saviour" (Lk.1:46,47). Safely delivered of her Son, she rejoiced in faith of the mighty deliverance He would work for her soul. The angels of heaven rejoiced as they sang of "good tidings of great joy" (Lk.2:10), even if they could not comprehend the mystery of which they sang (cf. I Pet.1:12). Peasant shepherds were filled with God glorifying praise, and their lives were never the same again, as a result of what they saw, heard and experienced in the field and in the stable on the first Christmas morning (Lk.2:20). There was more than the pursuit of science or the tracking of a star in the coming of the Magi to Bethlehem, there was faith. Their enquiries at the royal palace together with the stated reason for their coming, and the gifts they carried, witnessed to that. They expected to find a unique Child-King, were not disappointed, "were glad when they saw the Lord". They returned home spiritually liberated, heirs of salvation (Matt.2:1-12). Significantly, they presented gifts, the rich giving to the poor Who had made them supremely wealthy with the treasures of His grace (II Cor.8:9). Truly, Christmas is a time of "feasting and joy, of sending portions one to another, and giving gifts to the poor"; for those for whom it means salvation from the Lord, a season of "light and gladness, and joy and honour" (Esth.8:16).

ACCORDING TO PURPOSE
IX
THE WARD OF PROVIDENCE

Mordecai and Haman are the hero and villain respectively of the Book of Esther. When placed side by side these two characters are seen to have much in common. Both aspired to greatness, and each was equipped intellectually to attain and cope with it. Both were urgent and meticulous in the making and executing of their plans, had the ability to recruit the services of those necessary to the accomplishment of their schemes, and both were eqully ruthless when dealing with those they considered enemies. It is not surprising that, being cast together in the same scene on the stage of time, they should clash and the one should eliminate the other. Having set their sights on the same goal, it was impossible for them to co-exist. Considered from the purely human standpoint the one was as the other, neither was an individual to be lightly crossed or opposed. Yet, Mordecai had the edge on the other, was the victor, and we find ourselves thinking, "That is as it should be". Why? Differences are apparent in the two also. Mordecai is more appealing, more gracious, seen to be motivated by humanitarian, nationalist and spiritual aims, whereas Haman is self-centred and self-seeking — advancement for his own sake is all that matters. We like Mordecai, consider that he is the better man by reason of breeding, personality and character. But true as that is it does not account for the difference and triumph. Mordecai, basically the same as Haman, and if left alone heading for the same fate, has been made different by God. By the alchemy of grace the base metal of his character has been transformed into fine gold. The beginnings of this transformation were when God adopted Mordecai into the family of grace and made him a child of God.

Adoption is one of the great doctrines of grace associated with our salvation and is one of the fruits of redemption as wrought by Jesus Christ. This is of the greatest possible comfort to all men and women of faith. It is defined succinctly and comprehensively by the Shorter Catechism: "Adoption is an act of God's free grace, whereby we are received into the number, and have the right to all the privileges, of the sons of God" (Ans.34). Here we need not concern ourselves with the mechanics of adoption but with the fact as known to us through faith. That it is an act of God's free grace means that we have been brought into a favoured position as God's children not by any natural right, merit or deserving man might pretend to lay claim to. It is an act of God, "with whom there is no variableness, neither shadow of turning", conferred upon us independently of what we were, and therefore irrevocable. It is a being brought into His family, given His name and endowed with all the privileges membership of His family entails, that makes us all the same in His eyes, "heirs of God, and joint heirs with Christ", our Redeemer. Put another way: adopted by grace we can consider ourselves the wards of Providence.

A ward is invariably a child who is defenceless and in need of protection, who is needy and requires provision, who is bereft of parents or their love and wants a guardian, and who receives all that from one willing and able to take the responsibility. Esther is a typical example. She lost both her parents when young and would have been exploited by the unscrupulous, unwanted and neglected by the unloving, had not her uncle, Mordecai, consented to be her guardian. He adopted her as his own daughter and she became his ward. We read frequently of a child being made a ward of court. Perhaps he was a tug-of-love baby, each divorced or separated parent squabbling over the right of guardianship. The child is torn between the two and suffers in many ways. The law intervenes and he is placed in the care of the courts until a satisfactory solution to the problem is found. During the period he is a ward of court, such resources of the State as are deemed necessary being utilized to provide him with the security and care he has been deprived of.

That was Mordecai. Original sin had orphaned him, stripping him of all the natural defences against spiritual wickedness that abounded on all sides, robbing him of access to the provision which nurtures the soul in righteousness, and left him alone and frightened, the butt of all the conflicting forces which were abroad. None cared for his soul and his situation was desperate until the courts of heaven intervened. God covenanted to be a father to him and make him His son, and to be his all in time and for eternity. Included among the benefits of this adoption are the promise that physical and temporal needs will be met (Matt.6:28-34), that protection and care will be available twenty-four hours every day (Ps.121:3,4), that a suitable portion of the good things of this life will be forthcoming (cf. Prov. 13:22,25) together with the prospect of discipline lovingly, wisely, justly administered (Heb. 12:6). As is well known, not all the children of God receive the above blessings in equal measure. They are given to, or with-held from, each at the discretion of God, and in order that they might contribute to the making of each child what his heavenly Father desires. They are the blessings of Providence controlled by a thoughtful, good and gracious hand. The receiving of them makes each child of God what Mordecai was, a ward of Providence.

He who exposes himself to danger in the cause of truth and when maintaining standards of righteousness has a sure defence in his God. It is one of the benefits of being a ward of Providence. When Mordecai refused to give to Haman the worship and reverence due to God alone, he knew he was disobeying the king's command and was inviting the venomous sting of Haman's hatred. But Haman considered a single Jew too small a fish for him to angle after; he would bide his time and have the pleasure of executing vengeance on the entire captive Jewish people which would include Mordecai. What sweet revenge that would be! But it was the Providence of God at work. During Haman's proposed waiting period Mordecai was left unmolested, free to keep his conscience clean before God and his fellowmen in a sober, righteous and godly manner; and, of course, free to plan a counter attack when Haman finally declared his intentions. Moses was the recipient of the same protection. Sent to negotiate the deliverance of Israel from Egypt, he stood repeatedly in the presence of Pharaoh unarmed, not to beg but to demand the release of his people. Yet, surrounded as Pharaoh was by his bodyguard and constantly frustrated and humiliated by the thrust of Moses' demands, displays and refusal to compromise, never once did he threaten Moses with arrest or death. It was as though an unseen wall separated them, and an unseen power was at work restraining Pharaoh's penal powers to ensure Moses' safety. This unseen force was the Providence of God. When Moses, the prophet with the inferiority complex, came before the king, he came with a dignity and spoke with an authority he did not feel, but the monarch saw and heard, was impressed and treated Moses as an equal. It was God's doing (Ex.7:1). Also, the ease with which Pharaoh found he could extricate himself and his land from the various plagues, the last one excepted, convinced him that Moses' bark was worse than his bite, that sooner or later Moses must run out of ideas and they would be back where they started, and with Israel more firmly enslaved. Most likely, that was the argument with which he silenced his councillors who, undoubtedly, clamoured for Moses' arrest; for when the plagues increased in severity and effect, they demanded as an alternative to their pleas for Moses' apprehension, "How long shall this man be a snare unto us? Let the men go that they may serve their God; knowest thou not that Egypt is destroyed?" (Ex. 10:7). In other words, if you will not listen to us and immobilise this terrorist, at least get him and his peasants beyond our borders before it is too late. The blindness and stubbornness of a despot was God's protection for His servant. Of course, the Lord's servants are often humiliated, embarrassed and frequently suffer physical violence in the pursuit of their vocation. David and Paul are outstanding examples of this. David outlawed and hunted as a wild beast by Saul, often in situations where there was but a step between him and death, nevertheless emerged from all to become king and to continue on the throne until the Davidic dynasty was established. From his youth his life was a long series of providences which ensured his deliverance and safety. What Paul endured in the service of the gospel is catalogued for us in II Corinthians chapter 11. What is recorded there suggests that he was blessed with an iron constitution in order to endure the severest of hardships, and that he led what the world would term a charmed life. Here is the story of unrecorded miracles of escape from one danger and calamity after another, all of which, including his physical resilience, must be attributed to the Providence of God; a statement which is supported by the account of his shipwreck during the voyage to Rome found in Acts chapter 27, verses 14 to the end. Whether it was Mordecai or Moses or David or Paul, each followed the spiritual way as laid down in First Peter. They did not return evil for evil or railing for railing, but were prepared to bless them that despitefully used them, knowing that being followers of that which is good, none could harm them; "for the eyes of the Lord are over the righteous, and his ears are open to their prayers; while the face of the Lord is against them that do evil" (I Pet.3:8-13). They were the wards of Providence.

It is a sore point with many Christians - indeed, as it was with some of the penmen of Scripture - that as far as the material, the temporal and the physical are concerned the non-Christian seems to fare much better. This was particularly painful to Old Testament believers because their Scriptures equate prosperity with godliness, affluence with righteousness, the former in each case being the token of the Lord's approval, the blessing which accompanies piety and devotion to God. Many among the wicked do flourish as a green bay tree, while scores of Christians do go from one adversity to another and never seem to prosper; but the contrary can be stated both of many who have no place for God and of great numbers of God's children. Further, that a man spurns the law of God and never seems to be in the troubles others find themselves in does not mean that he is happy, satisfied or contented. His prosperity could be a millstone around his neck, a burden the carrying of which denies him inner peace and blessing, a commodity powerless to supply the qualities he knows his life is lacking; and all that so belied by outward appearances that he is the envy of multitudes. Seeing him strutting around proud as any peacock, many wished that they walked in Haman's shoes, but within the secret of his house we find him complaining, "All (my prosperity) avails me nothing, so long as I see Mordecai the Jew sitting at the king's gate" (Esth.5:13). Like Haman, Ahab the king was as miserable as if he were a pauper, because he could not have Naboth's vineyard (I Kgs.21:4-6). For the unrighteous there is always a fly in the ointment of prosperity which makes it stink. Whereas, many Christians never having known prosperity do not miss it or want it, considering the little that they have plus the peace of God as a pearl of great price inhabiting their breasts affluence enough for them; while other believers, fluctuating between prosperity and adversity, like Paul have learned that whatsoever state they are in therewith to be content, and prove that godliness with contentment is great gain (Philip.4:11; 1 Tim.6:6). True prosperity is to know the blessing of God and that no Christian need ever be without. It is the hallmark of those who are the wards of Providence.

However, the Book of Esther points to an equally exciting truth, namely, that when God's judgments fall on the unrighteous, as fall they must, their prosperity is transferred to the righteous. When Haman fell from favour, his estates were given over to Esther who entrusted their care to Mordecai, and the position of prominence Haman had occupied at court became Mordecai's (Esth.8:1,2,15). It would be easy to dismiss this as a one off thing, the accident of a peculiar set of circumstances without parallel in Scripture and unknown in the annals of the Church. But on reflection, it is seen to be a principle of divine operation at work on behalf of all who have the right to be called the children of God. It is one which is enunciated in Scripture. Job says, "This is the portion of a wicked man; though he heap up silver as dust, and prepare raiment as the clay, he may prepare it but the just shall put it on, and the innocent shall divide the silver" (Job 27:13, 16,17). The Book of Proverbs speaks in a similar vein: "The wealth of the sinner is laid up for the just" and "he that by usury and unjust gain increaseth his substance, he shall gather for him that will pity the poor" (Prov.13:22; 28:8). The Preacher adds his contribution when he writes, "To the sinner (God) gives travail, to gather and to heap up, that he may give to him that is good before God" (Eccl.2:26). The conquest of Canaan illustrates this principle. It was a fertile land and by the industry of the inhabitants was most productive. They contributed greatly to its wealth and for centuries lived prosperously from its bounty until the vileness of their religious immorality and practices brought the judgments of God showering upon them. The Israelites overran them and fell heirs to the milk and honey with which the land flowed. With the minimum of effort they entered the country and immediately partook of what they had not laboured for. We read, "They did eat of the old corn of the land, and the manna ceased on the morrow after they had eaten of the old corn of the land" (Josh.5:11,12).

The principle may be explained from the teaching of Jesus Himself in His parables of the talents and the pounds. In each of these parables the servant who hid what had been given him to use was condemned for his lack of foresight, initiative and endeavour; and what he refused to use was transferred to the servant who had employed most energetically and enthusiastically what had been entrusted to him. This was a move which surprised Jesus' hearers and brought a protest from them. This He quickly silenced saying, "For unto every one that hath shall be given, and he shall have abundance; but from him that hath not shall be taken away even that which he hath" (Matt.25:25,28; Lk.19:24-26). These parables are concerned with service within the kingdom of God, but the judgment pronounced on the two unfaithful servants falls with equal force on those who within the field of Providence hoard what they have for their own selfish ease. For here also whatever a man has has been given by God in order that it might be used for the recipient's good, the benefit of society, and in a manner which will bring glory to God within a caring community. If it is used wrongly or not at all, it is lost to the person concerned but not to God. The Lord cannot and does not tolerate waste. What one fails to do another by the maximum use of what he has will make his responsibility and accomplish. So doing, he both develops and increases the talents he possesses and finds an added extra to do what others failed to attend to. That was true literally of Mordecai in relation to Haman. The wealth and the estates of the latter were hoarded and misspent on the selfish concerns of their possessor, but when vengeance overtook him, all that was his was handed over to the superintendance of Mordecai, a man who had employed diligently and faithfully all that had been granted to him. He put it to work as Haman should have done, so confirming the truth of the proverb, "He that by usery and unjust gain increaseth his substance, he shall gather it for him that will pity the poor" (Prov.28:8). Mordecai's epitaph was, "Mordecai was great among the Jews, and accepted of the multitude of his brethren, seeking the wealth of his people, and speaking peace to all his seed" (Esth.10:3). Being in the right place and at the right time and, like David the king before him, "behaving himself wisely", he prospered as the ward of Providence.

The road to this prosperity was not an easy one, but it was the way Providence ordained. As with Joseph and David before him, there would be times when Mordecai despaired of having his true worth recognised and of reaching the goal he felt was his; but the slowness of the pace and the disappointments and setbacks were all part of the care a benign Providence was bestowing upon him. In company with his two famous predecessors not only was he being led along a strange road to honour, but he was honoured as he walked it. The dignity, the graces and virtues with which he would adorn the office which awaited him were not merely developed by the trauma of the 'wilderness' life he lived, but were displayed to the fullest advantage by it. As the disappointments and the injustices which came Joseph's way revealed him to be a man of sterling integrity, and the hardships which haunted David brought to light the regal conduct of the man after God's own heart, and with which he would later grace the throne of Israel, so the qualities of statemanship, compassion and trustworthiness shone from him inspiring confidence. During the waiting period when he was virtually unknown, and frequently ignored or passed over, a minor official in a not too important ministry, Mordecai was known to his colleagues as what he eventually became, one worthy of the highest accolades in the service of the country. So it proved to be. When "Mordecai went forth from the presence of the king in royal apparel of blue and white, and with a great crown of gold", there is added the significant statement, "and the city of Shushan rejoiced and was glad" (Esth.8:15). The community was thrilled with the news that a great evil had been eliminated, that the right appointment to high honour had been made, that he who was worthy had come to his proper place and that it augered well for the future. But it must not be assumed that from then on it was plain sailing. What was referred to above as Mordecai's epitaph records that the qualities which made and kept him buoyant in foul weather were the same which made him seaworthy in the waters of political responsibility. "He lived happy ever after" might be the appropriate sentence with which to end a fairy tale, but the Book of Esther does not belong to that category. Mordecai would delight in his high office, deriving satisfaction and pleasure from it, but it required the constant exercise of all that had brought him to greatness to keep him great. Long working hours, short breaks for rest and recreation, a constant vigil against intrigue, a perpetual preparation of programmes for the fostering of national prosperity and prestige, an ever willing availability to cope with the unexpected crises which would occur from time to time, and an alertness to ensure that the interests of justice were served and none was exploited, were some of the demands which continued to test, to develop and to display the qualities by which he had come to power, and which kept him there until he heard the call, "Well done, good and faithful servant; thou hast been faithful over a few things, I will make thee ruler over many things; enter thou into the joy of thy Lord" (Matt.25:21). It is no light thing being a ward of Providence, but it is singularly rewarding.

That last note which was sounded, "the joy of the Lord," leads to a discussion of another aspect of the blessings which are the lot of the wards of Providence. Not all the children of God attain to prominence in this life, but none is outwith our heavenly Father's care, and all benefit from His gracious providences. Because we do, this other aspect we have in mind applies with equal force to each of us as to the Mordecais of this world. The Shorter Catechism's definition of adoption with which we commenced this chapter speaks of the privileges to which this grace gives us the right, and a few of them, particularly those appertaining to our study of Providence, were enumerated. But, obviously, these do not exhaust the list. As part of the whole family of God in heaven and on earth and whose final destination is the united family in heaven, the providential mercies we are never without are designed to keep us travelling heavenward, to bring us to heaven and have within themselves that which savours of heaven. This threefold blessing is what the wards of Providence have pre-eminently. That may be gleaned from the testimony of those who first received the promise of inheriting Canaan.

As has been observed already, Hebrews chapter 11 informs us that Abraham, Isaac and Jacob understood Canaan to be a type of heaven, three men travelled in and out of this promised land without actually occupying it or possessing anything in it except a cemetery; yet, we never read of them doubting the promise or giving way to discontent because they never seemed to get any nearer to the right of possession. They believed God and were convinced that they were journeying closer to it every day. They believed also that should death overtake them before gaining possession — and such were God's revelations to Abraham particularly, he did not expect the promise to materialise in his lifetime - that by death they would by-pass the earthly Canaan to enter into the heavenly. That knowledge gave a new perspective to the providential blessings which took them in and out of the promised inheritance and kept them in the ways of faith. Those fathers of Israel saw them as the preserving, sustaining, directing mercies that were bringing them on their way to heaven. Consequently, for them the providential took on a heavenly, spiritual character. That is both the beauty and strength of Providence for all who like the Patriarchs consider themselves pilgrims and strangers on the earth.

For the wards of Providence its mercies contain a foretaste of heavenly felicity. To him who with the eye of faith sees the towers of the Celestial City standing shrouded by the mists of this life on the horizon of time, the "all things" of his experience bring to his soul the thrill of the anticipation of the bliss that awaits him. Like Job he might have his share of the ills of this life and might bemoan the fact that "man is born to trouble as the sparks fly upward" (Job 5:7); but those troubles, so often likened to dark valleys, may be considered also as mountain top experiences. It might be a cold, wind swept, barren peak, but standing there it is possible to have a glimpse of what shall be. Is that mountain top the cold barrenness of poverty? Through the gloom can be seen the prepared resting place in the Father's house with its inexhaustible supplies which ensure that there there shall be neither hunger nor thirst. On that hill top are the arid winds of sickness, persistent ill-health or infirmity making life feel like a dry stick and death a destructive fire? That uncomfortable vantage point gives a sight, though as through a glass darkly, of the life which knows nothing of sickness or sorrow, and where death itself is unknown. Perhaps the gales of persecution or the whining chill of a sense of failure are making the footholds up there in the heights unsure and are giving one the impression of being forlorn or forsaken or useless. But there the interaction of light and shade as the sun struggles to shine through the clouds portrays the likeness of a cross stretching out into the far distance and at the head of which a golden crown is seen glistening faintly through the murkiness. It reminds the beholder that if we suffer with the Saviour, we shall reign with Him also. To have such experiences is to stand upon the peak of adverse providences and exclaim with Paul, "Our light affliction, which is but for a moment, works for us a far more exceeding, eternal weight of glory, while we look not at the things which are seen, but at the things which are not seen; for the things which are seen are temporal, but the things which are not seen are eternal" (II Cor.4:17). Bitter providences sweetened with the honey of heaven.

Pleasant providences have a similar sweetness. When in moments of quiet reflection it is recalled how God has blessed "in basket and store", that life has been without the absence of any good thing, that the lines of existence have been in pleasant places, the mind is immediately projected to a realm that is fairer than day. The pastoral beauty of the river of life, banked by an avenue of the trees of life which monthly bear the most luscious fruits, is a scene which makes the most breath-taking panorama of earthly beauty fade into insignificance, a realm where the extremes of heat and cold never cause discomfort. How gratefully the earthly is laid hold of as a pledge of the blessedness that is to be. When the heart ponders all the way that the Lord has led and acknowledges that it was a sure, a safe, and a right way, great are the longings which throng the soul. Such leadings inspire a prevision of the Lamb Who is in the midst of the throne leading the glorified on and on into the untarnished and untarnishable delights of heaven. "Oh, what must it be to be there!" There is in every providence, whatever its character, the perfume of heaven which can eliminate the sourness from this life and make its commonplace goodness exotic by its ability to bring home to the heart the glory of our unseen home.

Under its benign care the ministry of Providence prepares the children of God for heaven. As what Joseph, Moses and David experienced schooled, tempered and equipped them for the positions they ultimately occupied, so too whatever our lot, and whatever befalls us, contribute to what we shall be hereafter. Looking back on his wartime experiences, Sir Winston Churchill wrote, "I felt as if I were walking with destiny, and that all my past life had been but a preparation for this hour and this trial". Providences are sanctifying influences. Without holiness no man shall see the Lord, and, if we are prepared to be submissive to the divine will directing our way, this holiness is beaten into the soul on the anvil of time by the hammers of circumstance. Affliction is the fire which makes the soul responsive to the hammer. Loss is the striking off of whatever is excessive and unnecessary to the life and a hindrance to holiness. The shocks, disappointments and alarms which strike from time to time are the wielding of the hammer by a skilful hand. All shape and form the soul into the design planned for it. But fierce heat and blows are just part of the process. Repeatedly the soul is taken from the heat, the barrage of blows and the anvil and plunged into the cooling, soothing waters of life's delights, stays there for a time, and then the whole process is repeated with a greater or lesser intensity. By such means our heavenly Father imparts to His children the health and the strength, the firmness and robustness, the form and beauty of which the Lord Jesus is the pattern. It is the moulding of the soul into a holiness like unto Christ's, the sanctification of which the New Testament says so much, the developing of the nature so essential to life in heaven.

That is not to imply that before he exits from this life the Christian has reached a stage of perfection which makes him fit to enter heaven or even that his entrance is dependent on his state of holiness. The sincere Christian soul honestly striving to apprehend that for which he has been apprehended by Christ Jesus, knows that the first of these alternatives cannot be and that the second is not true. Whatever stage of spiritual development the Christian finds himself in, he knows that within himself there dwells no good thing, that the corpse of sinful flesh is still attached to him, that when he sees the gap which separates his attainments from the holiness of Christ, he must consider himself the very foremost of sinners. Were his entrance into the paradise of God dependent upon his spiritual attainments, he knows he could never get there. On his passing from this world the gates of glory will be swung open to him by the nail pierced hand of his Saviour, and he will have an abundant entrance because, and only because, the blood and righteousness of Jesus alone are his beauty, his glorious dress. Nonetheless, Providence is preparing him now for heaven. When the good soldier of Jesus Christ is confronted with the temptations of this life and, having put on the whole armour of God, overcomes them; when difficult and costly decisions have to be made, and made in the knowledge that they are the right ones; when there is a prompt response to the responsibilities, duties and demands of life, not occasionally but constantly; when God is loved with heart and soul and mind and strength and neighbours as oneself, then the will of God is being done on earth as it is in heaven. These are the preparations for the life hereafter. When the goodness of Providence permits - and how often it does - Christians to meet in fellowship and for worship, praise and instruction in truth and righteousness and for prayer, it is, apart from being essential to our spiritual well being now, a preparation for entering into the pleasures which are forevermore at God's right hand. The more gladly the privileges of Christian fellowship are seized and entered into, the more blessed will they be where there is no need of a temple. Included also among the pleasures which give fullness of joy at the Father's right hand are the beauties and activities of heaven which have their counterpart in this life. The Psalmist exulted in the marvels of creation. "The heavens declare the glory of God, and the firmament sheweth his handiwork," he sang (Ps. 19:1). The sights and sounds and movements of God's universe filled him with a great sense of wonder, gave to him intense aesthetic and spiritual pleasure which called from him volumes of praise and thanksgiving, as his poetry shows. Such wonders and delights are a faint reflection of the architectural glories of the realms of the blessed, and the privilege of revelling in their beauty must be one of the chief delights which are forevermore. Truly, the lines are fallen unto Christians in pleasant places, and to delight in all that the Creator's hand has provided is a thrilling preparation for the sights that gladden in that other world. The same might be said of the various talents with which the children of God in common with others are endowed and the pleasure which their use gives to the possessor and to his fellows. Each has at least one talent, and to use it aright is to have a wonderful sense of accomplishment and satisfaction, is to convey to friends, colleagues and neighbours a benefit they can appreciate, and adds to the sum total of happiness and usefulness to be found in the world. According to our differing abilities there is delight in composing, playing and listening to great music, writing and reading the classics of literature, painting and admiring the wonderful works of art, as there is in expressing and responding to the more homely talents which make for domestic bliss and enliven the community. These talents the children of God carry with them into heaven and there exercise them in ways they never dreamed possible, ways which glorify the giver of them, the God of heaven and contribute to the blessedness which is enjoyed there. Surely it is unthinkable that these abilities which are so much a part of the individual here perish in the grave with the body. Our talents perfected are very much part of each glorified personality, and to make the utmost use of them now is a fitting preparation for the life above.

Providence leads the children of God to heaven. There are times when it seems that the contrary is the case, when many who are older in the faith are tempted to say with the poet, "I am farther off from heaven, than when I was a boy". It is a sensation not unknown to the most mature. Job cried in an agony of spirit, "Oh, that I knew where I might find him!" (Job 23:3). He had lost God, life had lost its meaning and purpose. He seemed not to be getting or going anywhere. David, anointed to be king of Israel but banned as an outlaw, complained, "There is but a step between me and death" (I Sam.20:3). He was a man whose only destination seemed to be the grave. Elijah prayed that he might die, "for," said he, "I am no better than my fathers" (I Kgs.19:4). They had achieved nothing and got nowhere, and he was following in their footsteps. All that was the despair of men in the depths of spiritual depression, a malady from which few are immune, and when it grips the soul all sense of purpose flees and with it the hope of heaven recedes. If the goals of life are not reached, can heaven? But the Lord has His ways of reassuring His loved ones and of lifting them out of their slough of despond. With regard to the three cases just mentioned, they reached that to which they were called and to heaven also. Like the Israelites in the wilderness they were led by a way which they knew not, a road often full of doubt and dread but which led to the Promised Land.

The ever changing providences which are the believer's lot are for him the way home. That is the theme of the twenty-third Psalm. A psalm of pilgrimage it opens with the awareness that David, the shepherd, is the sheep of the Good Shepherd, Jehovah Himself. From that moment onward there is for him a safe passage "through all the changing scenes of life, in sorrow and in joy", led by his Lord and followed by goodness and mercy to dwelling in the house of the Lord forever. When passing through the comfort and plenty of the green pastures and living waters, or walking in the ways of chastisement and correction, or travelling through the dread valley of affliction, or perhaps when standing still, knowing security and supply in a time of persecution or opposition, or when wounded and exhausted by the journey and there savouring the healing and the reviving of the medicines of grace, and in each and all of these experiences he has the assurance that ever present is He Who gave His life for the sheep. That His vigilance is never relaxed for an instance is to know a happiness which is full and running over. All that carries the conviction that one is on the right way, the homeward way. At any given moment it is possible to stop and reflect that as light gives way to darkness and darkness to light, as joy is supplanted by sorrow and sorrow is replaced by joy, as health is replaced by sickness and sickness by health, as relaxation follows labour and labour recreation, as excitement and boredom alternate, as youth advances into manhood and manhood to age, these are but the scenery, the landmarks, the sign posts which identify the way to the Father's house. Were the number and variety of providences missing, were it all gusting wind and rain, hail, snow and sleet, or were it all brilliant sunshine with its accompanying drought and barrenness, there would be ample reason for considering oneself lost. But the way which is marked with the blood stained footprints of the Shepherd, while it might be circuitous, at times torturous and constantly up and down hill, is the way where His goodness and love flow unrestrainedly to all who follow Him, ever impressing upon His sheep that this is the only way, the surest way, the quickest way to the heavenly fold. That knowledge quickens and footsteps of faith, make the sheep more sure footed, permits them to expect and receive the grace they need to take each step and to pass through each phase of the journey, and every night "pitch their moving tent a day's march nearer home".

None is as favoured as the wards of Providence.